PERIOD OF ADJUSTMENT

OR HIGH POINT IS BUILT ON A CAVERN

A SERIOUS COMEDY
BY TENNESSEE WILLIAMS

For tenderness I would lay down
The weapon that holds death away,
But little wordss of tenderness
Are those I never learned to say.

★

★

DRAMATISTS
PLAY SERVICE
INC.

TO THE DIRECTOR AND THE CAST

PERIOD OF ADJUSTMENT was presented by Cheryl Crawford at the Helen Hayes Theatre in New York City on November 10, 1960. It was directed by George Roy Hill; the stage settings and lighting were by Jo Mielziner. The cast, in order of appearance, was as follows:

RALPH BATES ....James Daly

ISABEL HAVERSTICK .... Barbara Baxley

GEORGE HAVERSTICK ....Robert Webber

SUSIE ....Helen Martin

MRS. MC GILLICUDDY ....Nancy R. Pollock

MR. MC GILLICUDDY ....Lester Mack

POLICE OFFICER ....Charles Mc Daniel

DOROTHEA BATES ....Rosemary Murphy

THE SCENE

The action of the play takes place in Ralph Bates' home in a suburb of a mid-southern city. The time is Christmas Eve.

PERIOD OF ADJUSTMENT

or

High Point is Built on a Cavern

ACT I

The set is the interior and entrance of a "cute" little Spanish-type suburban bungalow. Two rooms are visible onstage, the living room with its small dining alcove and the bedroom: there are doors to kitchen and bath. A bit of the stucco exterior surrounds the entrance, downstage right or left: a Christmas wreath is on the door: above the door an ornamental porch light, or coach-lantern, with amber glass or possibly glass in several colors. The fireplace in the fourth wall of the set is represented by a flickering red light. Of course, the living room contains a TV set with its back to the audience, its face to a big sofa that opens into a bed. The dog is a cocker spaniel. There's a rather large Christmas tree, decorated, with child's toys under it and a woman's fur coat in an open box, but no child and no woman. Ralph Bates, a boyish-looking man in his middle thirties, is approaching the TV set, at proscenium facing upstage, with a can of beer and opener.

AT RISE: *Ralph is seated on a very high stool downstage glaring at the TV, a can of beer in his hand.*

TV COMMERCIAL. [*Sound No. 1*] 'Twas the night before Christmas and all through the house Not a creature was stirring except Mother Mouse! (*Ralph slides off stool and picks up fireplace poker.*) Light and lively as she could be, Her smile as bright as the Christmas tree! (*Ralph pokes at fireplace.*) Why is she lively? Why is she light? Her dishes are washed by MIRACLE BRIGHT!

RALPH. *No snow*, Mother Mouse. (*Crosses L. to chair and sits. Fire flickers brighter on D. C.*)

TV VOICE. —That's right, what is it that lights up a house? Electric light bulbs? Oh, no! It's the smile on the face of Mom when —— (*Ralph crosses to TV, kneels front of it. He changes channels four times, [Sound No. 2] turns it down to a faint whisper and rushes to front door, switching on the porch light, which is a coach lantern of red and amber glass. A bar of "White Christmas" on TV [Sound No. 3]. Crosses to chair. TV sound down at sound of approaching car—car honking. [Sound No. 4] It's snowing: Flakes are projected across him as he goes out on the paved terrace. Muffled shouts below.*)

RALPH. (*Crosses to terrace.*) Hey, there, boy! Drive 'er up under the car-port!

GEORGE. (*Texas voice—Off L.*) Whacha say, boy?

RALPH. PUT 'ER UNDER THE CAR-PORT!

GEORGE. Wheels won't catch, too steep!

RALPH. Back her all the way out and then shoot 'er up in first!

ISABEL'S VOICE. (*High-pitched with strain—Off L.*) Will you please let me out, first, George! (*Car door is heard. [Sound No. 5] Ralph crosses to dinette, gets rice, crosses behind door L. Isabel enters L., waits at door.*)

RALPH. Yeah, come on in, little lady. (*Isabel enters. Goes R. toward sofa. He throws rice at her. She ducks the bombardment with a laugh that's more like a sob.*)

ISABEL. (*Crosses D. R.*) Oh, no, please! I never want to see rice again in my life, not uncooked anyhow —— (*Crosses front of fire.*) That fire looks wonderful to me. I'm Isabel Crane, Mr. Bates. (*Removes gloves and extends hand.*)

RALPH. I thought you'd married that boy. (*Both speak in deep Southern voices: hers is distinctly Texas.*)

ISABEL. I mean Mrs. George Haverstick. (*She says her new name with a hint of grimness.*)

RALPH. (*Crosses to door, shouts to George at car.*) Wait'll I put m'shoes on, I'll come out! (*This shout is unheard—He crosses to D. stool, puts on shoes.*)

ISABEL. You have a sweet little house.

6

RALPH. (*With a touch of amiable grimness.*) Yeah, we sure do —— (*Shoes on, crosses to door.*) Wheels cain't git any traction, 'stoo damn steep. (*Crosses L. to door. Shouts down.*) LOCK IT UP, LEAVE IT OUT FRONT!—I guess he's gonna do that, yep, that's what he's doin', uh-huh, that's what he's doin' . . .

ISABEL. (D. C.) Does it snow often in Nashville?

RALPH. No, no, rarely, rarely. (*Crosses to stool. Ties shoes. Gives her a glance. Ralph has a sometimes disconcerting way of seeming either oblivious to a person he's with or regarding the person with a sudden intense concentration as if he'd just noticed something startling or puzzling about them. But this is a mannerism that the actor should use with restraint.*)

ISABEL. (D. C.) It was snowing all the way down here, it's my first acquaintance with snow. I'm from Sweetwater, Texas.

RALPH. Oh, a little Texas girl.

ISABEL. It's my first real acquaintaince with snow. Except for one little flurry of snow in Saint Louis the day befo' Thanksgivin' day, this is my first real acquaintance with, with—with a real snow . . . What *is* he doing down there? (*Indicating outside.*)

RALPH. He's unloadin' th' car.

ISABEL. I just want my small zipper bag. Will you please call down to him that's all I want of my things?

RALPH. (*Shouting. Crosses to door.*) Leave all that stuff till later. Ha ha. I didn't know you could get all that in a car.

ISABEL. Surely he isn't removing our wedding presents! (*Crosses to terrace.*) Is he *insane*, Mr. Bates? (*Crosses to door.*) George! Just my small zipper bag, not everything in the car! Oh, Lord. (*Retreats from door. Crosses into c. of living room.*) He must think we're going to *live* here for the rest of our *lives!* He didn't even warn you all we were coming.

RALPH. He called me up from West Nashville.

ISABEL. Yes, just across the river.

RALPH. (*At door, looking out.*) What is that car, a Caddy?

ISABEL. It's a fifty-two Cadillac with a mileage close to a hundred and twenty thousand. It ought to be retired with an old-age pension, Mr. Bates.

RALPH. (*At door.*) It looks like one of them funeral limousines.

ISABEL. (*Crosses to his R. at door. Wryly.*) Mr. Bates, you have hit the nail on the head with the head of the hammer. That is just

7

what it was. It's piled up a hundred and twenty thousand miles between Burkemeyer's Mortuary and various graveyards serving Greater Saint Louis. GAWGE, CAN YOU HEAR ME, GAWGE? Excuse me, Mr. Bates. (*She slips past him onto terrace again.*) GAWGE, JUST MY SMALL ZIPPER BAG. (*Weeps.*) I give up, Mr. Bates. (*Weeping turns to laugh.*)

RALPH. (*Still chuckling at door.*) What's he want with a funeral limousine? On a honeymoon trip?

ISABEL. I asked him that same question and got a very odd answer. He said there's no better credit-card in the world than driving up at a bank door in a Cadillac limousine. (*Tries to laugh. She crosses by him, enters house, crosses C., then crosses to sofa, sits.*) Oh, I don't know, I—love Spanish-type architecture, Spanish mission-type houses, I—don't think you ought to stand in that door with just that light shirt on you, this is a—such a—*sweet* house . . . (*She seems close to tears. Something in her tone catches his attention and he comes in, closing the door.*)

RALPH. (*Crosses to her, L.*) Ha, ha, well, how's it going? Is the marriage in orbit?

ISABEL. Oh! (*Tries to laugh at this, too.*) Will you please do me a favor? Don't encourage him, please don't invite him to spend the night here, Mr. Bates! I'm thinking of your wife because last night—in Cape Girardeau, Missouri?—he thought it would be very nice to look up an old war-buddy he had there, too. He sincerely thought so, and possibly the war-buddy thought so, too, but NOT the wife! Oh, no, not *that* lady, no! They'd hardly got through their first beer-cans with—remembrances of Korea, when that bright little woman began to direct us to a highway motel which she said was only a hop, skip and jump from their house but turned out to be almost across the state-line into—Arkansas? (*George enters L., deposits 2 suitcases on porch, exits.*) Yaias, Arkansas, I think I can take this off, now! (*Removes a muffler. Ralph takes it from her and she murmurs "Thanks."*) Mr. Bates, I did tell him that this is one night of the year when you just don't intrude on another young married couple.

RALPH. Aw, come off that, little lady! Why, I been beggin' that boy ever since we got out of the service to come to Nashville. He had to git married to make it. Why, every time I'd git drunk, I'd call that boy on the phone to say "Git to hell down here, you old Texas jack-rabbit!" And I'd just about given up hope he'd ever

8

show! (*He crosses to door, puts muffler on rack, opens door.*)
Hey! (*He sees bags.*) *Hey!*

ISABEL. (*Rises, starts across to him.*) *What?!*

RALPH. Ha ha ha! He put these bags at the door and run back
down to the car.

ISABEL. (*At his* R.) *What* did he ——?!

RALPH. Gone back down for more luggage. (*He picks up bags,
starts in.*) I'll take these in.

ISABEL. (*Retreating* L., *backwards as he advances with bags.*)
Those are *my* pieces of luggage! All but the little blue zipper bag
which is all that I wanted! (*Ralph sets bags down* U. *of sofa.*)
[*Sound No. 6*]

RALPH. (*Calling out open door.*) *Hey!*

ISABEL. *What?!*

RALPH. (*He runs to door, she follows him.*) *Hey, boy!* He's
gotten back in the car an' driven off, ha ha! (*Steps onto porch.*)

ISABEL. *Driven!? Off!?* Did you say? (*Pause. He looks off, then
backs, laughs.*) My heavens. You're right, he's *gone!* (*Ralph stum-
bles and mumbles.*) Mr. Bates, he's *desposited* me on your hands
and driven away. (*She is stunned.*) Oh, how *funny!* Isn't this
funny! (*Laughs wildly, close to sobbing.*) It's no *surprise* to me,
though! All the way down there from Cape Girardeau where we
spent our wedding night, Mr. Bates, I had a feeling that the first
chance he got to, he would abandon me somewhere! (*She crosses
into living room, he follows, closes door.*)

RALPH. Aw, now, take it easy!

ISABEL. (*She crosses between stool and sofa.*) That's what he's
done! Put me and my bags in your hands and run away.

RALPH. (C.) Aw, now, no! The old boy wouldn't do that, ha ha,
for Chrissakes. He just remembered something he had to, had
to—go and get at a—drug store.

ISABEL. If that was the case wouldn't he mention it to me?

RALPH. He mentioned it to me.

ISABEL. When? When? He just called up from the car.

RALPH. Aw now, I known that boy a long time and he's always
been sort of way out, (*He crosses* U. *to suitcases, picks them up.*)
but never way out that far!

ISABEL. (*She crosses* L. *to chair, crying.*) Where is your wife,
where's Mrs. Bates?—Mr. Bates?

RALPH. Oh, she's not here, right now.

9

ISABEL. (*Crying.*) I'm such a FOOL! Oh, I'm such a *fool!* —Why didn't I know better, can you answer me that? He brought up everything but the little blue zipper bag which is all I asked faw!—It had my, all my, (*Sits.*) it had my—*night* things in it . . .

RALPH. (*He sets down bags u. of sofa, crosses to her.*) Let me get you a drink.

ISABEL. Thank you, no I don't drink . . .

RALPH. It's never too late to begin to.

ISABEL. Where is your wife, Mr. Bates?

RALPH. (*He moves bags under table R. of sofa.*) Oh, she's—not here, now, I'll tell you about that later.

ISABEL. She will be outraged: this is one night of the year when you don't want outside disturbances—on your hands . . .

RALPH. (*Picks up wrapped brandy bottle from table, crosses to her. Opens package.*) I think I know what to give you.

ISABEL. I did expect it but yet I didn't expect it!—I mean it occurred to me, the possibility of it, but I thought I was just being morbid.

RALPH. (*He crosses u. behind her with bottle, puts corkscrew in.*) Aw, now, I know that boy. We been through two wars together, took basic training together and officer's training together. He wouldn't ditch you like that unless he's gone crazy.

ISABEL. (*Rises, crosses u. 3 steps to C.*) George Haverstick is a very sick man, Mr. Bates. He was a patient in Neurological at Barnes Hospital in St. Louis, that's how I met him. I was a student nurse there.

RALPH. (*Crosses D. to her R. with bottle.*) Yeah? What was wrong with him in the hospital, honey?

ISABEL. If we see him again, if he ever comes back to this house, you will *see* what's wrong. *He shakes!* Sometimes it's just barely noticeable, just a constant, slight tremor, (*He crosses D. above stool to open bottle.*) you know, a sort of—vibration, like a—like an electric vibration in his muscles or nerves?

RALPH. Aw. That old tremor has come back on him, huh? He had that thing in Korea. (*Hands her drink.*)

ISABEL. (*She steps D. Refuses drink.*) How bad did he have it in Korea, Mr. Bates?

RALPH. You know—like a heavy drinker—except he didn't drink heavy.

ISABEL. (*She speaks with a prim severity like an outraged spinster which is quite incongruous to her pretty, childlike appearance.*) Yes, well—it's much worse than that now. It's like he had St. Vitus Dance, Parkinson's disease, but it isn't Parkinson's disease. It's no disease at all.

RALPH. What in hell is it then?

ISABEL. THAT is a MYSTERY! He shakes, that's all. He just shakes. Sometimes you'd think that he was shaking to pieces. (*She crosses to door, hears car, opens it. [Sound No.7]*) —Was that a car out front? (*He crosses to her.*) No! I've caught a head-cold, darn it. (*Blows nose. She crosses* C.) When I met Mr. George Haverstick —— Excuse me, you're watching TV!

RALPH. (*He closes door. Crosses down to TV, turns it off, then sits on stool* C.) Naw, I'm not watchin' TV.

ISABEL. (*She crosses* U. *opposite front door.*) I'm so wound up, sitting in silence all day beside my—silent bridegroom, I can't seem to stop talking now, although I—hardly know you. Yes, I met him at Barnes Hospital, the largest hospital in Saint Louis, where I was taking my training as a nurse, he had gone in Barnes instead of the Veterans Hospital because in the Veterans Hospital they couldn't discover any physical cause of this tremor and he thought they just said there wasn't any physical cause in order to avoid having to pay him a physical disability— (*She crosses to chair, sits.*) compensation!—I had him as a patient on the night shift at Barnes Hospital. My, did he keep me running! The little buzzer was never out of his hand. Couldn't sleep under any kind of sedation less than enough to knock an elephant out!—Well, that's where I met George, I was very touched by him, honestly, very, very touched by the boy! I thought he sincerely loved me. I don't suppose another man could see George the way I saw him, so handsome, so afflicted, so afflicted and handsome . . . Yes, I have caught a head cold, or am I crying? (*He pulls out handkerchief, gives it to her.*) I guess it's fatigue—exhaustion.

RALPH. You're just going through a period of adjustment.

ISABEL. Of course at Barnes he got the same diagnosis, or lack of diagnosis, that he'd gotten at the Vets' Hospital in Korea and Texas and elsewhere, no physical basis for the tremor, perfect physical health, suggested—psychiatry to him! He blew the roof off! You'd think they'd accused him of beating up his grandmother, at least, if not worse! I swear! (*She crosses to door, looks out.*)

11

Mr. Bates, (*Above chair.*) I still have sympathy for him, but it wasn't fair of him not to let me know he'd quit his job until one hour after our marriage. He gave me that information after the wedding, right after the wedding he told me, right on the bridge, Eads Bridge between Saint Louis and East Louis, he said: Little Bit? Take a good look at Saint Louie because it may be your last one! I'm quoting him exactly, those were his words. (*She steps front of chair, sits.*) I don't know why I didn't say drive me right back . . . Isn't it strange that I didn't say turn around on the other side of this bridge and drive me right back? I gave up student nursing at a great hospital to marry a man not honest enough to let me know he'd quit his job till an hour after the wedding!

RALPH. Gawge is a high-strung boy.—But they don't make them any better.

ISABEL. A man's opinion of a man!—If they don't make them any better than Gawge Haverstick they ought to stop production! (*Ralph throws back his head, laughing heartily.*) No, I mean it, if they don't make them better than a man that would abandon his bride in less than—how many hours?—On the door-step of a war-buddy and drive on without her or any apology to her, if that's the best they make them, I say *don't make them!* (*He crosses u. to bar, pulls out cork, pours brandy into snifter, takes glass and beer can, crosses to fire, sets glass and can on TV. Then he uses bellows on fire. As he works bellows, fire flickers. She crosses down and sits on pouf.*) Did Gawge tell you on the phone that he's quit his job?

RALPH. What job did he quit, honey?

ISABEL. He was a ground-mechanic at Lambert's Airfield in Saint Louis. I had lost my job too. I didn't exactly quit, no, I was politely dismissed. My first day in Surgery?—I *fainted!*—when the doctor made the incision and I saw the blood, I keeled over . . .

RALPH. That's understandable, honey.

ISABEL. Not in a nurse, not in a girl that had set her heart on nursing, that —— (*She looks at his watch.*) How long has he been gone?

RALPH. Just a few minutes, honey: Christmas Eve traffic is awful heavy an' Gawge being Gawge, he may have —— How long have you known Gawge?

12

ISABEL. I'm afraid I married a stranger.

RALPH. (*He warms snifter over fire.*) Everybody does that.

ISABEL. Not my parents. Daddy and Momma worshipped each other for 35 years. For 12 years before I was born. They'd given up hope of ever having a child when I came along and I guess their surprise and gratitude—made them spoil me a bit —— (*She rises, crosses to door, looks out.*)

RALPH. You'd been going steady how long?

ISABEL. Ever since his discharge from Barnes Hospital. Isn't this suburb called High Point?

RALPH. Yes. High Point over a cavern.

ISABEL. His place was in High Point, too. Another suburb called High Point, spelled Hi dash Point—hyphenated.

RALPH. I guess all fair-sized American cities have got a suburb called High Point, hyphenated or not, but this is the only one I know of that's built right over a cavern.

ISABEL. Cavern? Well, I said, George, on the bridge, (*She crosses D. R. of chair.*) we're not driving down to Florida in that case. We're going to find you a job, we're going from city to city until you find a new job and I don't care if we cross the Rio Grande, we're not going to stop until you find one! Did I or didn't I make the right decision? In your opinion, Mr. Bates.

RALPH. Well. How did he react to it?

ISABEL. Stopped talking and started shaking! So violently I was scared he would drive that funeral car off the road! Ever since then it has been hell. (*There is a low rumble. [Sound No. 8] A picture falls off the wall.*) What was that? (*She jumps up.*)

RALPH. (*Crosses R. to picture.*) Oh, nothing. We get that all the time here because this suburb, High Point, is built over a great big underground cavern and is gradually sinking (*Rehangs picture.*) into it: an inch or two a year. (*Pause—Crossing to her R.*) Why don't you take off your coat and sit back down by the fire? That coat keeps the heat off you, honey. (*She removes coat. He hangs it up by front door.*) —That boy's comin' back. (*Observing with solemn appreciation the perfect neatness of her small body.*) I'm *sure* that boy's coming back. (*She takes off jacket, he hangs it up.*) I am now *positive* of it! (*She crosses to fire, he follows to her R., kneels.*) That's a cute little suit you're wearing. Were you married in that, honey?

13

ISABEL. Yes, I was married in this little travelling suit. Appropriately.

RALPH. You couldn't look any prettier in white satin. (*He lights snifter with long match.*)

ISABEL. Thank you Mr. Bates. What is, what are you ——?

RALPH. Something to warm up your insides, little lady.

ISABEL. Well, isn't that sweet of you? Will it burn if I touch it?

RALPH. (*He hands her snifter, she takes it.*) Naw, naw, naw, take it, take it.

ISABEL. Beautiful. Let me hold it to warm my hands first, before I —— I'm not a drinker, I don't think doctors or nurses have any right to be, but I guess *now*—I'm out of the nursing profession! So . . . (*She drinks. He moves up to bar.*) —What a sweet little bar. What a sweet little house. And such a sweet Christmas tree.

RALPH. Yeah. Everything's sweet here.

ISABEL. Where is your wife Mr. Bates?

RALPH. My wife has quit me.

ISABEL. No! You're joking, aren't you?

RALPH. She walked out on me this evening when I let her know I'd quit my job.

ISABEL. (*Beginning to listen to him.*) Surely it's just temporary, Mr. Bates.

RALPH. Nope. Don't think so. I quit my job and so my wife quit me. (*He crosses to chair, sits. She comes to R. of stool.*)

ISABEL. I don't think a woman leaves a man as nice as you, Mr. Bates, for such a reason as that.

RALPH. Marriage is an economic arrangement in many ways, let's face it, honey. Also the situation between us was complicated by the fact that I worked for her father. But that's another story. That's a long other story (*He rises, crosses above stool.*) and you got your mind on George.

ISABEL. I think my pride has been hurt.

RALPH. (*Crosses D. to her.*) I told you he's coming back and I'm just as sure of it as I'm sure Dorothea isn't. Or if she does, that she'll find me waiting for her. Ohhhhh, noooooo! (*Crosses out to terrace. She follows.*) I'm cutting out of this High Point Over A Cavern on the first military transport I can catch out of Nashville.

ISABEL. (*Vaguely—crossing to terrace.*) You don't mean that, Mr. Bates, you're talking through your hat, out of hurt feelings,

14

hurt pride. (*She opens the front door and stands looking out forlornly as a lost child. She really does have a remarkably cute little figure and Ralph takes a slow continual and rather wistful stock of it with his eyes.*)

RALPH. I got what I had comin' to me, that I admit, for marryin' a girl that didn't attract me.

ISABEL. Did you say didn't attract you?

RALPH. Naw, she didn't attract me in the beginning. She's one year older'n me and I'm no chicken. But I guess I'm not the only man that would marry the only daughter of an old millionaire with diabetes and gallstones and one kidney. Am I? But I'm telling you I'm convinced there is no greater assurance of longevity in this world than one kidney, gallstones an' diabetes! That old man has been cheating the undertaker for yea many years. Seems to thrive on one kidney. (*Tosses beer-can down the terrace.*)

ISABEL. Do you always throw beer-cans on your front lawn, Mr. Bates?

RALPH. (*Turns D.*) Never before in my life. I sure enjoyed it.

ISABEL. (*She sits on bench.*) It's nice out here.

RALPH. (*Looks off L.*) George is gonna be shocked when he sees me. I sacrificed my youth to ——

ISABEL. What?

RALPH. Yep, it's nice out here. I mean, nicer than in there.

ISABEL. You sacrificed your youth?

RALPH. Oh, that. Yeah! I'll tell you more about that unless it bores you.

ISABEL. No.

RALPH. She had fallen into the hands of a psychiatrist when I married this girl. This phychiatrist was charging her father fifty dollars a session to treat her for a condition that he diagnosed as "psychological frigidity." She would shiver violently every time she came within touching distance of a possible boy-friend. Well —I think the psychiatrist misunderstood her shivers.

ISABEL. She might have shivered because of ——

RALPH. That's what I *mean*! Why, the night I met her, I heard a noise like castanets at a distance. I thought some Spanish dancers were comin' on! Ha ha! Then I noticed her teeth.—She had buckteeth at that time which were later extracted!—Were chattering together and her whole body was uncontrollably shaking!

15

ISABEL. We both married into the shakes! But Mr. Bates, I don't think it's very nice of you to ridicule the appearance of your wife.

RALPH. Oh, I'm not!

ISABEL. You WERE!

RALPH. At my suggestion she had the buck-teeth extracted. It was like kissing a rock-pile before the extractions! I swear! (*Pause: he looks at her, away.*)

ISABEL. Now, Mr. Bates.

RALPH. (*Pause: looks again, away.*) This snow almost feels warm as white ashes out of a—chimney. (*He looks at her, she turns away. She crosses* U. *through door to sofa, sits. He follows, closing door. At her* L.) Yep, her old man was payin' this head-shrinker fifty dollars per session for this condition he diagnosed as "psychological frigidity." I cured her of that completely almost overnight. But at thirty-seven, my age, you ain't middle-aged but you're in the shadow of it and it's a spooky shadow. I mean, when you look at *late* middle-aged couples like the McGillicuddys, my absent wife's parents . . .

ISABEL. (*Rises, crosses by him to chair, sets snifter by phone, turns back to him* L. *of stool.*) Mr. Bates, don't you think I should go down-town and take a hotel room? Even if Gawge comes back, he ought not to find me here like a checked package waiting for him to return with the claim check. (*Susie enters by porch,* L. *Comes to door.*) Because if you give up your pride, what are you left with, really? (*Susie knocks.*)

RALPH. Here he is now. You see? COME ON IN, LOVER BOY! (*Suzie knocks again.*) THAT DOOR AIN'T LOCKED! (*He crosses to door, opens it.*) What can I do fo' you, Susie? (*Susie enters with a sheepish grin.*)

SUSIE. 'Scuse me for comin' to the front door, Mr. Bates, but that snow's wet and I got a hole in muh shoe! (*She enters, crosses* R. C.)

RALPH. Come on in. They sent you for somethin'?

SUSIE. Yes, suh, they sent me faw th' chile's Santie Claus.

RALPH. (*To her, after closing door.*) Aw, they did, huh? Well, you go right back an' tell the McGillicuddys that "the chile's Santie Claus" is stayin' right here till the chile comes over for it, because I bought it, not them, and I am at least *half* responsible for the "chile's" existence, *also*. Tell them the chile did not come into the world without a father and it's about time for the chile to acknowledge that fact and for them to acknowledge that fact and

(He crosses to door, opens it, looks, then looks back.) —How did you git here, Susie?

SUSIE. Charlie brought me.

RALPH. Who's Charlie?

SUSIE. Charlie's they new *showfer*, Mr. Bates.

RALPH. Aw. Well, *(She follows Ralph to porch—he leads her out.)* Tell my wife and her folks, the McGillicuddys, that I won't be here tomorrow but "the chile's Santie Claus" will be here under the tree and say that I said Merry Christmas.

SUSIE. Yes, suh.

RALPH. Can you remember all that?

SUSIE. Yes, suh. *(Turns and shouts.)* Don't come up, I'm comin' right down, Charlie! *(She exits L. Sound of a car starting below the terrace as Susie withdraws. [Sound No. 9] Ralph looks out of the open door till the car is gone. Then he closes door, crosses C., then crosses D., sits on stool.)*

RALPH. Dig that, will yuh? Sent a colored girl over to collect the kid's Christmas! This is typical of the Stuart McGillicuddys. I'd like to have seen Mr. Stuart McGillicuddy, the look on his face, when that Western Union messenger give him my message of resignation this afternoon and he was at last exposed to Ralph Bates' true opinions of him!

ISABEL. You should have let her take the child's Christmas to it.

RALPH. *(Rises, crosses U. R., then turns D.)* They'll be over. Don't worry. And will I blast 'em! Think of the psychiatrist fees that I saved her fat-assed father! I even made her think that she was attractive, and over a five-year period, got one pay-raise when she give birth to my son which she has turned to a sissy. *(Crosses D. to stool, sits. Isabel hasn't listened to his speech.)*

ISABEL. I thought that was George at the door . . .

RALPH. *(Rises, crosses to bar, opens beer can.)* That's life for you.

ISABEL. *(To him.)* What?

RALPH. I said isn't that life for you!

ISABEL. *(She crosses D. to sofa, sits.)* *What* is life for us *all*? *(Sighs.)* My philosophy professor at the Baptist college I went to, he said one day, "We are all of us born, live and die in the shadow of a giant question mark that refers to three questions: Where do we *come* from? *Why? And where, oh, where* are we going!" *(Pause.)* . . . What? *(She looks up.)*

RALPH. (*He picks up Xmas tree lights.*) Nothing.

ISABEL. Well!

RALPH. (*He rises crosses D. to TV. Pause: then:*) D'you like Christmas music?

ISABEL. Everything but "White Christmas."

RALPH. (*Crosses back sofa, sits.*) Aw, y' don't like "White Christmas"?

ISABEL. The radio in that car is practically the only thing in it that *works!* We had it on all the time. Conversation was impossible, even if there had been a desire to talk! It kept playing "White Christmas" because it was snowing I guess all the way down here, yesterday and—today . . .

RALPH. A radio in a funeral car?

ISABEL. I guess they played it on the way back from the graveyard. (*He rises, crosses D. to fire, kneels, works bellows.*) Anyway, once I reached over and turned the volume down. He didn't say anything, he just reached over and turned the volume back up. Isn't it funny how a little thing like that can be so insulting to you? Then I started crying and still haven't stopped! I pretended to be looking out the car window till it got dark. (*He crosses to L. of stool.*)

RALPH. (*He crosses to her R., leans back on stool.*) You're just going through a little period of adjustment to each other.

ISABEL. I don't know, Mr. Bates, I wish I did but I don't. . . . (*She rises, opposite him.*) What do you do with a bride left on your doorstep, Mr. Bates?

RALPH. Well, I, *ha ha!*—never *had* that experience!

ISABEL. Before! Well, now you're faced with it, I hope you know how to handle the situation.

RALPH. (*Obliquely investigating.*) Where did you spend last night?

ISABEL. (*She turns away to L. Vaguely.*) Where did we spend last night?

RALPH. Yeah. Where did you stop for the night?

ISABEL. (*Rubbing her forehead and sighing with perplexity.*) In a, in a—oh, a tourist camp by the name of the—Old Man River Motel? Yes, the Old Man River Motel.

RALPH. (*He sits on stool, faces D.*) That's a mistake. The first night ought to be spent in a real fine place regardless of what it cost you. It's so important to get off on the right foot. If you get

18

off on the wrong foot, it can take a long time to correct it. (*Nods in slow confirmation of this opinion.*) Um-hmmm. Walls are built up between people a hell of a damn sight faster than—broken down. (*Pause. She sits sadly by the fireplace. Sound of car going by house.*) [*Sound No. 10*] —What went wrong last night? (*He leans foward to her.*)

ISABEL. (*She stiffens.*) —Let's not talk about that.

RALPH. I don't mean to pry into such a private, intimate thing, but ——

ISABEL. No, let's don't!—I'll just put it this way and perhaps you will understand me. In spite of my being a student nurse, till discharged—my experience has been limited, Mr. Bates. Perhaps it's because I grew up in a small town, an only child, too protected. Daddy was very strict but devoted. He didn't allow me to date till my last year at High and then my father insisted on meeting the boys I went out with and laid down pretty strict rules such as when to bring me home from parties and so forth. If he smelled liquor on the breath of a boy? At the door? That boy would not enter the door! And that little rule ruled out a goodly number.

RALPH. I get the picture. It figures. Now I'm going to tell you something about your boy. That boy George Haverstick always bluffs about his ferocious treatment of women. Always did in the service. To hear him talk you'd think he spared them no pity! However, I happened to know he didn't come on as strong with those dolls in Tokyo and Hong Kong and Korea as he liked to pretend to. Because I heard from those dolls. He'd just sit up there on a pillow and drink that rice wine with them and teach them *English!* Then come downstairs from there, hitching his belt and shouting, "*Oh, man! Oh, brother!*" like he'd laid 'em to waste.

ISABEL. (*Turns away.*) That was not his behavior in the Old Man River Motel.

RALPH. What went wrong in the Old Man River Motel?

ISABEL. Too many men think that girls in the nursing profession must be—*shock*-proof. I'm not, I wasn't—last night . . .

RALPH. Oh. Was he drunk?

ISABEL. He'd been drinking all day in that heaterless retired funeral hack in a snowstorm to keep himself warm. Since I don't drink, I just had to endure it. Then, we stopped at the Old Man River Motel, as dreary a place as you could find on this earth! The electric heater in our cabin lit up but gave off no heat! Oh,

19

George was comfortable there! Threw off all his clothes and sat down in front of the heater as if I were not even present.

RALPH. Aw.

ISABEL. Continuing drinking.

RALPH. Aw.

ISABEL. Then began the courtship, and, oh, what a courtship it was, such tenderness, romance! I finally screamed. I locked myself in the bathroom and didn't come out till he had gotten to bed and then I—slept in a chair . . .

RALPH. You wouldn't ——

ISABEL. Mr. Bates, I couldn't, I just couldn't! The atmosphere just wasn't right. And he —— (*Covers her face—crying.*) —I can't tell you more about it, just now except that it was a nightmare, him in the bed, pretending to be asleep, and me in the chair pretending to be asleep too and both of us knowing the other one *wasn't* asleep and, and, and—I can't tell you more about it right now, I just can't tell more than I've told you about it, I ——

RALPH. Hey! Let me kiss the bride! Huh? Can I kiss the bride?

ISABEL. You're very kind, Mr. Bates. I'm sure you were more understanding with your wife when you were going through this ——

RALPH. —period of adjustment? Yeah. That's all it is, it's just a little—period of adjustment. (*He bestows a kiss on her tearstained cheek and a pat on her head.*)

ISABEL. (*Holding his hands to her face.*) It isn't as if I'd given him to believe that I was experienced: I made it clear that I *wasn't.* He knows my background and we'd talked at great *length* about my—inhibitions which I know are—*inhibitions,* but—which an understanding husband wouldn't expect his bride to overcome at *once,* in a tourist cabin, after a *long—silent—*ride:—in a *funeral* back in a *snowstorm* with the *heater* not working in a—*shocked!* *condition!*—having just been told that—we were *both* unemployed, and —— (*A car is heard driving up outside. [Sound No. 11] Ralph rushes to the door.*)

GEORGE. HEY!

RALPH. HEY! (*Isabel catches her breath, waiting, waiting!*) Ha ha! (*Isabel expels her breath and sits down. Ralph, shouting through snow.*) *Your wife thought you deserted her!* (*Car door slams.*) [Sound No. 12]

20

GEORGE. (*From distance.*) *Hey!* (*George enters* L., *with champagne.*)

BOTH TOGETHER. Powder River—One mile wide and two inches deep! (*George sets champagne on railing.*)

RALPH. You ole son of a tail gun!

GEORGE. Ha ha! Yeah, I'm a tail gunner, alright. (*George and Ralph start to shake then embrace, George points to Ralph's balding head, Ralph pushes him into room where he sees Isabel.*)

RALPH. How'sa Texas jack-rabbit?

GEORGE. Well, I see you still got yuh dawg.

RALPH. Yeah, I got my dawg because m' wife's folks are cat-lovers.

GEORGE. (*Takes off coat, throws it on chair by Xmas tree.*) You'll get your wife back tomorrow.

RALPH. Hell, I don't want her back.

GEORGE. Y' don't want 'er back?

RALPH. That's right.

GEORGE. (*Rolling up sleeves.*) Hell, in that case, you won't be able to beat 'er off with a *stick*, ha ha! Won't be able to beat her away from the door with a stick t'morrow . . .

ISABEL. I doubt that Mr. Bates means it.

GEORGE. Didn't you all have a kid of some kind? I don't remember if it was a boy or a girl.

ISABEL. The toys under the tree might give you a clue ——

GEORGE. Huh?

ISABEL. —as to that.

RALPH. Yeah, it's a boy—I guess. Beer? (*Ralph crosses by George to bar—George and Isabel look at each other, then:*)

GEORGE. You bet.

ISABEL. How old is your little boy?

RALPH. Three years old and she's awrready made him a sissy.

GEORGE. They'll do it ev'ry time, man.

RALPH. (*Ralph opens beer can. Crosses* D. R. *of stool—George follows to his* R. *Ralph gives George beer.*) I didn't want this kind of a dawg, either. I wanted a Doberman-Pinscher, a dawg with some guts, not a whiner! But she wanted a poodle and this flop-eared sad sack of a spaniel was a compromise which turned out to be worse'n a poodle, ha ha . . .

GEORGE. I'll bet yuh dollars to doughnuts your wife and kid'll be back here tomorrow.

RALPH. They won't find me here if they do. I'm all packed to go. I would of been gone when you called but I'm waitin' t' git a call from a boy about to git married. I want him to come over here an' make a cash offer on all this household stuff since I spent too much on Christmas and won't be around to collect my unemployment.

GEORGE. Come along with us. We got a big car out there an' we're as free as a breeze. Ain't that right, Little Bit?

ISABEL. Don't ask me what's right. I don't know! I *do* know, though, that couples with children don't separate at Christmas, and, George, ——

GEORGE. Well how about it, huh?

ISABEL. —let your friend work out his problem himself. You don't know the situation and don't have any right to interfere in it. And now will you please go get my little blue zipper bag for me? *Please!*

RALPH. (*To George as if she hadn't spoken.*) Naw, I'm just going out to the Army air-field a couple miles down the highway and catch the first plane going west.

GEORGE. We'll talk about that.

ISABEL. (*Imploring.*) *George!*

GEORGE. (*He runs out to porch, gets champagne bottle, closes door, tosses bottle to Ralph, just missing Isabel.*) AW, HERE! I forgot to give you your present! After drivin' almost back into Nashville to find a liquor store open.

RALPH. (*Catching bottle.*) Lover Jesus, champagne!?

GEORGE. Imported and already cold.

RALPH. (*Glancing at Isabel.*) I knew he was buyin' me something? She thought you deserted her, boy.

ISABEL. *All right, I'll get it myself!* (*Runs to door, opens it, exits.*) *I'll go out and get it out of the car myself!* (*She rushes out into snow, leaving door open. George crosses* u. *to door, looks after her.*)

GEORGE. Boy, you an' me have got a lot to talk over.

CURTAIN

ACT II

They are at the same positions as at end of Act I, Ralph
D. R. *George at door.*

GEORGE. Oh man, oh brother. Have I got a lot to tell you.
(*He closes door, enters.*) Has she said anything yet?
RALPH. (*Above stool.*) Who?
GEORGE. Her.
RALPH. About what?
GEORGE. Me.
RALPH. Aw, about you, naw, not a word. She never mentioned
your name even. . . . Well how's it goin'? So far? (*He crosses
out to dinette with champagne bottle.*)
GEORGE. We'll talk about it *later*. Discuss it *throughly! Later!*
RALPH. Y' got married yestiddy mawnin'?
GEORGE. Yeah.
RALPH. How was last night? (*Isabel enters* L., *pushes open door,
crosses to George, leaves door open.*)
GEORGE. We'll talk about *that* later, too.
ISABEL. *I* can't break the lock on that car!
GEORGE. (*Crossing by her to close door.*) Little Bit, I didn't
know that you wuh bawn in a barn. (*He means she left the door
open again.*)
ISABEL. I didn't know a lot about you, either! Mr. Bates! Mr.
BATES. (*Ralph re-enters—crosses* D. *to Isabel, turns with a vague
smile to her.*) The gentleman I married refuses to get my zipper
bag out of the car or unlock the car so I can get it myself. (*Phone
rings.*) [Sound No. 13]
RALPH. (*Crosses to phone, picks it up. George crosses to bedroom, then crosses to sofa, sits. Isabel follows to above him.
Ralph—in a slow, hoarse drawl, at phone.*) Aw, hi, Smokey. I'm
glad you got my message. Look. I quit Regal Dairy Products and
I'm flyin' out of here late tonight or early tomorrow morning and I
thought maybe you might like to look over some of my stuff here,

23

the household equipment, and make me a cash offer for it. I'll take less in cash than a check since I'm not gonna stop at the Coast, I'm flying straight through to Hong Kong (*George rises, crosses to R. of Ralph.*) so it would be difficult for me to cash yuh check an' of course I expect to make a sacrifice on the stuff here. Hey! Would you like a beaver-skin coat, sheared beaver-skin coat for Gertrude? Aw. I'd let you have it for a, for a—third off! Aw, well, anyhow, come over right away, Smokey, and make me an offer in cash on as much of this household stuff as you figure that you could use when you git married. O.K.? (*Hangs up.*)

GEORGE. (*Puts arm around Ralph, with furtive glance at Isabel.*) Hong Kong!?

RALPH. Yeah.

GEORGE. (*Crossing c. with Ralph.*) Back to Miss Lotus Blossom in the Pavillion of Joys?

RALPH. I never had it so good. At least not *since*.

GEORGE. You remember——? (*He makes a suggestive gesture —they both laugh heartily at remembrance. George crosses u. to bar, Ralph crosses u. opposite front door.*)

ISABEL. (*Acidly. Between them from one to the other.*) Mr. Bates, your character has changed since my gypsy husband appeared! He seems to have had an immediate influence on you, and not a good one. May I wash up in your bathroom? (*They both look at her with slight, enigmatic smiles.*)

RALPH. What's that, honey?

ISABEL. Will you let me use your bathroom?

RALPH. (*He leads her to bedroom door.*) Aw, sure, honey. I'm sorry you——

GEORGE. (*Stepping down.*) Now what's the matter with her? (*Turns to Isabel.*) Now what's the matter with you?

ISABEL. (*To George.*) May I talk to you alone? In another room? (*She crosses into bedroom between beds.*)

RALPH. You all go in the bedroom and straighten things out. Oh, gimme the keys, George? (*George does. Ralph exits L.*)

GEORGE. (*At bedroom door.*) Now what's the matter with you?

ISABEL. Is this a sample of how I'm going to be treated?

GEORGE. (*Crosses D. opposite her at L.*) What do you mean? How have I treated you, huh?

ISABEL. I might as well not be present! For all the attention I have been paid since you and your buddy had this tender reunion!

GEORGE. Aren't you being a little unreasonable, honey?

ISABEL. I don't think so. I don't think it's really very unreasonable of me to want to be treated as if I LIVED! EXISTED! (*Ralph re-enters with bags, crosses* C., *listens.*)

GEORGE. Will you quit actin' like a spoiled little bitch? I want to tell you something. You're the first woman that ever put me down! Sleepin' las' night in a chair? What kind of basis is that for a happy marriage?

ISABEL. You had to get drunk on a highway! In a heater-less (*Ralph sets down bag at* U. *sofa, crosses to phone table—gets brandy, crosses to bar.*) funeral car after informing me you had just quit your job! Blasting my eardrums, afterwards, with a car radio you wouldn't let me turn down. How was I supposed to react to such (*Ralph picks up brandy glass, beer, crosses to bedroom door.*) kindness? Women are human beings and I am not an exception to that rule, I assure you! I HATED YOU LAST NIGHT AFTER YOU HAD BEEN HATING ME AND TORTURING ME *ALL DAY LONG*!

GEORGE. Torturing you, did you say? WHY DON'T YOU SIMMER DOWN! We ain't ALONE here, y'know!

RALPH. (*Crosses* D. *through door to above her.*) You all are just goin' through a perfectly usual little period of adjustment. That's all it is, I told her ——

GEORGE. Aw! You all have been talking?

ISABEL. What did you think we'd been doing while you were gone in that instrument of torture you have for a car?

GEORGE. You've got to simmer down to a lower boiling point, baby.

RALPH. (*Appealing to both of them.*) Just goin' through a period of adjustment . . .

ISABEL. Adjustment to what, Mr. Bates? Humiliation? For the rest of my life? Well, I won't have it! I don't want such an "adjustment." I want to —— May I— (*Sobs.*) —freshen up a little bit in your bathroom before we drive downtown? To check in at a hotel? (*George crosses to bedroom door.*)

RALPH. Sure you can.

GEORGE. I ain't goin' downtown—or checkin' in no hotel. (*George crosses* L.)

ISABEL. (*She follows George, to* C.) *You may do as you please!*

I'm checking in a hotel. (*She crosses back to bedroom, sits edge* U. *bed. George stops, turns toward* R.)

RALPH. (*Offering glass.*) You never finished your drink. (*George crosses to bar, sits on stool facing* D.)

ISABEL. I don't care to, thanks. Too many people think that liquor solves problems, all problems. I think all it does is *confuse* them!

RALPH. I would say that it—*obfuscates* them a little, but ——

ISABEL. Does *what* to them, Mr. Bates?

RALPH. I work crossword puzzles. I—ha ha!—pick up a lot of long words. Obfuscates means obscures. And problems need obfuscation now and then, honey. I don't mean total or permanent obfuscation, I just mean *temporary* obfuscation, that's all. (*He is touched by the girl and he is standing close to her, still holding the glass out toward her. He has a fine, simple sweetness and gentleness when he's not "bugged" by people.*) D'ya always say *Mister* to men?

ISABEL. Yes, I do till I know them. I had an old-fashioned upbringing and I can't say I regret it. Yes. (*She is still peering out the door at her new husband.*)

RALPH. I wish you would say Ralph to me like you *know* me, honey. (*Ralph crosses* U. *to door, closes it. George immediately opens it, then crosses to chair, sits on arm.*) You got a tension between you and tensions obfuscate love. Why don't you get that cross look off your face and give him a loving expression? Obfuscate his problems with a sweet smile on your face and ——

ISABEL. *You* do that! I'm not in a mood to "obfuscate" his problems. Mr. Bates, I think he'd do better to face them like I'm (*George crosses to bedroom door.*) facing mine, such as the problem of having married a man that seems to dislike me after one day of marriage.

RALPH. Finish this drink and obfuscate that problem because it doesn't exist. (*George switches on bedroom light, then crosses to stool* C., *leans against it, facing* D. *Ralph smiles tolerantly at this show of distrust which is not justified.*)

ISABEL. (*Recalling Ralph who has started after George.*) You have a sweet little bedroom, Mr. Bates.

RALPH. I married a *sweet, homely* woman. Almost started to like her. I cain like *anybody*, but ——

ISABEL. (*Crosses to dressing table. Sits.*) Mr. Bates? Ralph? This house has a *sweetness* about it!

RALPH. (*Crosses D. R. of her.*) You don't think it's "tacky"?

ISABEL. No. I think it's sweet!

RALPH. We got it cheap because this section of town is built right over a cavern.

ISABEL. (*At dressing table. Without listening.*) What?

RALPH. This High Point suburb is built over an underground cavern and is gradually sinking down in it. You see those cracks in the walls?

ISABEL. Oh . . . (*She hasn't listened to him or looked.*) Oh! My little blue zipper bag. May I have it?

RALPH. (*He crosses to U. door.*) She wants a little blue zipper bag.

GEORGE. (*Gets bag, throws it to Ralph who catches it. Isabel screams.*) Here, give it to her, goddam it! Now whatcha screamin' faw? (*George crosses to bedroom door.*)

ISABEL. (*Rises, crosses U. to Ralph, gets bag, puts it on D. bed.*) Thank heaven Mr. Bates is such a good catch. All my colognes and perfumes are in this bag including a twenty-five dollar bottle of Vol-de-nuit. Mr. Bates, will it be necessary for me to phone the hotel?

GEORGE. (*At door.*) Didn't you hear what I said?

ISABEL. Mr. Bates! Would you mind phoning some clean, inexpensive hotel to hold a room for us tonight?

GEORGE. I said I'm not gonna check in a hotel tonight!

ISABEL. Reserve a *single* room, please!

RALPH. Sure, sure, honey, I'll do that. Now you just rest an' fresh up an' —— (*Ralph crosses out of bedroom, takes George C., gets beer can from bar.*) Come on, George, let her alone here, now, so she can rest an' calm down.

GEORGE. Look at my hands! Willya look at my hands?

RALPH. What about your hands?

GEORGE. Remember that tremor? Which I had in Korea? Those shakes? WHICH STARTED IN KOREA?

RALPH. Aw, is it come back on yuh?

GEORGE. Are you blind, man?

RALPH. (*Crosses behind bar.*) Yeah. How's your drink?

GEORGE. (*Crosses to edge of bar.*) She in the bathroom yet?

RALPH. (*Looks into bedroom.*) Naw, she's still in the bedroom.

GEORGE. (*Crosses* L. *to door.*) Wait'll she gits in the bathroom so we can talk.

RALPH. What's your drink, ole son?

GEORGE. Beer's fine. (*Turns* R.) —Jesus! (*Crosses to bar.*)

RALPH. (*At bar.*) Rough?

GEORGE. Just wait'll she gits in the bathroom so I can tell you about last night. (*He crosses into bedroom, opposite her.*)

RALPH. Here. (*Offers him beer.*)

GEORGE. (*To Isabel.*) Little Bit, you told me you couldn't wait to get under a good hot shower. There's a good shower in that bathroom. Why don't you go and get under that good hot shower? (*He starts to exit, stops at door, comes back.*)

ISABEL. I have a lot to think over, George.

GEORGE. Think it over under a good shower in that bathroom, will you? I want to take a bath, too. (*He starts to exit again, stops.*)

ISABEL. (*Suddenly turning to face him from the bed.*) George, I feel so lonely! (*Pause: Ralph crosses to front door, opens it, looks out.*)

GEORGE. Yeah, and whose fault is that? Huh?

ISABEL. I don't know why I suddenly feel so lonely! (*Sobs again. He regards her coolly from door.*)

GEORGE. Little Bit, go in the bathroom and take your shower, so I can go take mine, or do you want us to go in and take one together? (*She rises indignantly, crosses to bathroom with bag. He shuts door behind her, crosses to Ralph in living room.*) Naw, I didn't think so. There now, she's in! (*He shakes both fists in air with a grimace of torment.*) Look! I got to get rid of that girl. I got to get rid of her quick. Jesus, I can't stay with that girl. You got to help me.

RALPH. (*Crosses* D. C. *to stool.*) Man, you're married to her.

GEORGE. You're married to one! Where's yours? You son of a tail gun! Don't tell me I'm married to her when we ain't exchanged five remarks with each other since we drove out of Cape Girardeau where she refused to —— (*He crosses to bedroom door, listens, closes it, then crosses to Ralph.*) Has she come out of the bathroom? No! Refused to even *undress!* But huddled up in a chair all night in a blanket, crying? Because she had the misfortune to be my wife?!

RALPH. I wouldn't count on it.

GEORGE. On what?

RALPH. Her thinking it's such a misfortune.

GEORGE. I described to you how we passed the night, last night!

RALPH. Is this girl a virgin?

GEORGE. She is a *cast-iron* virgin! And she's going to stay one!

RALPH. I wouldn't count on that.

GEORGE. I would. I count on it. First thing I do tomorrow is pack her onto a plane back to Saint Louie.

RALPH. You must have done something to shock her.

GEORGE. That's the truth, I tried to sleep with her.

RALPH. Maybe you handled the little lady too rough.

GEORGE. Now don't talk to me like a wise old man of the mountain about how to deal with a woman. Who was it had to make dates for who at Big Springs, Texas and who was it even had to make arrangements for you with those Tokyo dolls?

RALPH. That's not women, that's gash.

GEORGE. Gash are women.

RALPH. They are used women. You've got a unused woman and got to approach her as one.

GEORGE. She's gonna stay unused as far as I am concerned. (*Stoops by Xmas tree.*) Now what the hell is this thing you're fiddlin' with? (*He has crouched among toys under tree.*)

RALPH. Rocket launcher. Miniature of the rocket launchin' pad at Cape Canaveral.

GEORGE. No snow! How's it work?

RALPH. Gimme the count-down. I'll show you. (*George moves stool to sofa, Ralph sets launcher on floor* C. *They kneel by it, Ralph* L. *George* R.)

GEORGE. Ten. Nine. Eight. Seven. Six. Five. Four. Three. Two. oww! (*Rocket has fired in his face. Rocket retrieved, they get together, crossing* D. C. *Ralph* L. *of George.*)

RALPH. Ain't you got sense enough to stand clear of a rocket launcher? Ha ha! Last week, just last week, I caught the little bugger playin' with a rag doll. Well. I snatched that doll away from him an' pitched it into the fireplace. He tried to pull it out an' burned his hand! Dotty called me a monster! The child screamed, "I hate you!" an' kicked my shins black an' blue! But I'll be damned if any son of Ralph Bates will grow up playin' with dolls. Why, I'll bet you he rides that rockin' hawss side-saddle!

Naw, a sissy tendency in a boy's got to be nipped in the bud, otherwise the bud will blossom.

GEORGE. I would prefer to have me a little girl. (*He says this wistfully.*) Little girls prefer daddy. Female instinct comes out early in them.

RALPH. I wanted a boy but I'm not sure I got one. (*He crosses* u. *to tree, sets down rocket, then crosses* D. *to* R. *of George.*) However, I got him a real red-blooded boy's Christmas, at no small expense for a man in my income bracket! (*Isabel comes out of the bathroom. She wears robe and slippers, carries dress and bag and shoes. Sets them on* u. *bed.*) —I like the kid, I mean I—sure would suffer worse than he would if the neighborhood gang called him "Sissy!"

ISABEL. —Mr. Bates? (*Crosses to bedroom, opens door roughly, startling both of them.*)

GEORGE. (*Pause.*) Whaddaya want?

ISABEL. I called for Mistuh Bates.

GEORGE. Mistuh Bates, Mrs. Haverstick would like to talk to you, suh. (*Ralph crosses to bedroom, as George crosses* u. *to bar.*)

ISABEL. I just want to know if you have called the hotel.

RALPH. (*Entering.*) Sure, sure, honey. Don't worry about a thing. Everything's gonna be fine.

ISABEL. (*She is in a robe.*) Thanks, Ralph. You've been awf'ly kind to me. Oh! Could I help myself to some of this Pepto-Bismol I found in your sweet little bathroom?

RALPH. Aw, that pink stuff? Take it all. I never touch it. It's Dorothea's. She used to get acid stomach. I'll get you a glass of water. (*He crosses into bathroom.*)

ISABEL. It's very soothing. (*She crosses to dressing table. Sits. He re-enters with water, crosses to her. George crosses to bedroom door, head cocked, somewhat suspicious.*)

RALPH. Well, I cured her of that. I doubt that she's hit that Pepto-Bismol bottle once in the last five years. (*George crosses to stool, leans face* R.)

ISABEL. I rarely suffer from an upset stomach. Rarely as snow in Nashville. (*Laughs lightly.*) But the human stomach is an emotional barometer with some people. Some get headaches, others get upset stomachs.

RALPH. Some even git diarrhea.

ISABEL. (*She rises, crosses front* D. *bed.*) The combination of

30

nervous strain and (*Sees statue on dresser.*) —Oh! What's this? (*Picks up a gorgeously robed statue of the infant Jesus.*)

RALPH. Aw, that. (*George crosses to bedroom door.*) That's the Infant of Prague. Prague, Czechoslovakia?

ISABEL. Oh?

RALPH. It was discovered there in the ruins of an old monastery. It has miraculous properties.

ISABEL. Does it? (*George crosses to chair, sits.*)

RALPH. They say that it does. Whoever gives you the Infant of Prague gives you a piece of money to put underneath it for luck. (*Ralph crosses by her to dresser, shows her penny under statue.*) Her father presented this Infant to Dorothea so the piece of money was naturally *one penny*. It's s'posed to give you prosperity if you're not prosperous and a child if you're childless. (*He sits R. of her.*) It give us a child but the money is yet to come in, the money's just been goin' out. However, I don't blame the Infant of Prague for that, because ——

ISABEL. (*George crosses R. to her, sets down beer, then crosses to bedroom door.*) Mr. Bates? Ralph? You know, very often people can be absolutely blind, stupid, and helpless about their own problems and still have a keen intuition about the problems of others?

RALPH. Yeah?

ISABEL. There is such a tender atmosphere in this sweet little house, especially this little bedroom, you can almost—touch it, feel it! I mean you can almost *breathe* the tender atmosphere in it! (*George crosses U. to Xmas tree, then to bar wall.*)

RALPH. (*Rising—in a slow, sad drawl.*) The color-scheme in this bedroom is battleship grey. (*Crosses U. between beds.*) And will you notice the cute inscriptions on the twin beds? "His" on this one, "Hers" on that one? The linen's marked his and hers, too. Well. The space between the beds was no-man's land for awhile. Her psychological frigidity was like a, like a—artillery barrage!— between his and hers. I didn't try to break through it the first few nights. Nope. I said to myself, "Let *her* make the first move."

ISABEL. Did she? (*He crosses to her.*)

RALPH. What do *you* think?

ISABEL. I think she *did*.

RALPH. (*Puts arm around her.*) Right you are! (*Gives her a little congratulatory pat on the shoulder.*)

31

GEORGE. (*Crossing to bedroom door.*) Hey, what's this heart-to-heart talk goin' on in here?

RALPH. (*Rises, crosses* U. *to George. Chuckling.*) Come on out of here, boy. I got something to tell you. (*Leads George out.*)

GEORGE. (*Backing* L.) What were you up to in there?

RALPH. (*Advancing and imploring.*) Go in there, quick, before she gets dressed, you fool!

GEORGE. (*Shaking him off.*) I'll be damned if I will!

RALPH. (*Crossing* D. *to* TV.) I'll turn the TV on loud. (*Turns on* TV.) [*Sound No.* 14]

ISABEL. (*Getting dressed in bedroom until entrance. Calling out.*) I'll be dressed in a jiffy!

RALPH. (*Crosses* U. *to George.*) Go ON! You just got a jiffy!

GEORGE. Yeah, and I've got some pride, too. She put me down last night, first woman ever to put me down in ——

RALPH. (*Taking his arm.*) I know, you told me, GO IN! Lock the door and ——

GEORGE. (*Shaking him off.*) YOU go in! That's what you WANT to do! I never had a girl yet that you didn't want to take over. This time you're welcome. GO IN! Go BACK IN AND BREATHE THE TENDER ATMOSPHERE OF THAT—SWEET LITTLE BEDROOM.

RALPH. (*Backing off.*) Gawge? Hey!—You're *shakin'*, man, you're shakin' to pieces! What kind of a son of a bitch d'you take me faw?

GEORGE. (*To him.*) The kind which you are, which you always have been!

RALPH. She is right about you. You are not well, son. . . .

GEORGE. (*Attacking.*) Where d'ya git this "son" stuff! Don't call me "son."

RALPH. Then grow up, will yuh! (*Crossing to bar.*) What's your drink? Same?

GEORGE. Yeah . . .

RALPH. (*Crossing back with brandy bottle.*) You're shakin' because you want to go in that bedroom. GO IN! Take the bottle in with you! I'll sit here and watch TV till —— (*Isabel has put on her traveling suit. She comes into the living room, moving to below bar. George crosses to chair. Ralph, bearing* TV, *crosses* D. *to turn it off fast. Ralph seeing her.*) —Too late now! (*Ralph crosses to sofa, sits.*)

32

ISABEL. (U. C. *In a sweet Texas drawl.*) Mr. Bates? Ralph? It breaks my heart to see all those lovely child's toys under the tree and the little boy not here to have his Christmas.

RALPH. He's with his mother.

ISABEL. I know, but his Christmas is here.

RALPH. He's a mama's boy. He's better off with his Mama. (*He indicates that she should smile at George.*)

ISABEL. How are you feeling, now, George? (*George grunts and turns to the bar. Isabel makes a despairing gesture to Ralph. George wheels about abruptly, suspecting some dumb-play. Isabel laughs lightly, sighs deeply.*)

GEORGE. I thought you'd set your heart on a single hotel room tonight.

ISABEL. (*Stepping to him.*) George, you're shaking worse than I've ever seen you.

GEORGE. That's! Not your problem, that's my problem, not yours!

ISABEL. (*She turns away, U. C.*) Oh ——!

RALPH. (*Ralph crosses U. to her R. To Isabel.*) Honey? Come here a minute. (*Ralph whispers something to her.*)

ISABEL. Oh, no. NO!—Mr. Bates, you are confusing the function of a wife with that of a —— (*Ralph crosses to sofa, sits.*) I feel sorry, I feel very sorry for you not-so-young young men who've depended for love, for tenderness in your lives, on the sort of women available near army camps, in occupied territories! (*Steps down opposite Ralph.*) Mr. Bates? Ralph? (*Pause.*) —Ralph, why did you quit YOUR job? Did you get the shakes, too?

GEORGE. (*Rises, crosses C.*) Now don't get bitchy with him.

ISABEL. I WASN'T BEING BITCHY!

RALPH. She wasn't being bitchy. She asked a logical question.

ISABEL. (*Between them.*) Just a question!

GEORGE. (*Attacking her.*) Can't you mind your own business for a change? You got fired too, don't forget! All three of us here is jobless!

ISABEL. (*To him.*) I am not forgetting. (*Primly, with dignity.*) I am not forgetting a thing, and I have a lot to remember.

GEORGE. Good. I hope you remember it. *Memorize it!* (*He is getting tight.*)

ISABEL. (*Sniffling a little.*) I think I caught cold in that car.

GEORGE. Caught cold? Hell, you were born with a cold ——

ISABEL. (*To George.*) *Stop that!*

GEORGE. In your damn little ——

ISABEL. (*To Ralph.*) MR. BATES, MAKE HIM STOP!

RALPH. (*To her.*) Let him blow off some steam.

GEORGE. Incurable cold! You didn't catch it from me.

ISABEL. (*Crossing* D. *above* TV.) I wish you had shown this side of your nature before, just a hint, just a clue, so I'd have known what I was in for.

GEORGE. (*Crossing to* L. *of stool, and* L. *of her.*) What hint did you give *me*? What clue did *I* have to *your* nature?

ISABEL. (*Ralph crosses* D. *to stool, sits.*) Did I disguise my nature?

GEORGE. You sure in hell did.

ISABEL. In what *way*, tell me, please!

GEORGE. (*Crossing* L.) You didn't put the freeze on me at Barnes! (*To Ralph.* L. *of stool.*) She was nurse at Barnes when I went there for those tests? To find out the cause of my shakes? She was my night nurse at Barnes.

ISABEL. (*Crossing* U. *of Ralph.*) Oh, stop! Don't be so crude! How can you be so crude?

GEORGE. (*Crossing* U. L. *steps.*) She was my night nurse at Barnes and gave me those alcohol rubdowns at bed-time. (*Crossing* D. *2 steps.*)

ISABEL. (*Crossing* U. *2 steps.*) That was my job. I had to. (*Crossing* D. *2 steps.*)

GEORGE. (*Crossing* U. *2 steps.*) Hell, she stroked and petted me with her fingers like she had on a pair of silk gloves. (*Crossing* D. *2 steps.*)

ISABEL. This is insufferable. (*Crossing* R. *to bedroom.*) I am going downtown. (*Crossing* L. *below Ralph. Covers her face sobbing.*) Just give me car-fare downtown.

GEORGE. (*To Ralph.*) You remember those Jap dolls with silk gloves on their hands in Tokyo, Ralph? Hell, she could of given them Jap dolls lessons!

ISABEL. (*Steps back* R.) I DID NOT TOUCH YOUR BODY EXCEPT AS A NURSE HIRED TO DO IT! YOU KNOW I

DIDN'T! I DID NOT TOUCH YOUR BIG OLD LECHEROUS BODY.

GEORGE. (Over Ralph.) How'd you give me a rub-down without touching my body? Huh? I mean how could you give me rub-downs without touching my body?

ISABEL. (Turns up to Ralph.) Please, please. Mr. Bates? You believe me? He's making out I seduced him while I was his nurse.

GEORGE. I didn't say that. Don't say I said that. I didn't say that. I said you had soft little fingers and you knew what you were doing. She'd say, "Turn over." I couldn't turn over. I had to stay on my stomach, (George crosses U. to bar.) I was so damned embarrassed.

ISABEL. (Crosses D. to sofa, sits.) Ah,—I feel nauseated. What filth you have in your mind!

RALPH. (Comforting her, sitting U. of her.) Honey? Little Lady? Come over and sit here with me. All this will all straighten out. It's going to be all straightened out. (George knocks beer can off bar, retrieves it. Crosses to above Ralph.)

GEORGE. Oh, Jesus. Worse than ever, worse than ever before! How could I have kept that job? A ground mechanic with hands that can't hold tools?

ISABEL. Go take your tranquillizers. They're in my blue zipper bag.

GEORGE. Where's your blue zipper bag?

ISABEL. In the bedroom. (George crosses to bedroom, exits to bathroom with bag.)

RALPH. See, honey? That boy isn't well. You got to make some allowances for him. You're both nice kids, both of you, wonderful people. And very good-looking people. I'm afraid you're doomed to be happy for a long time together, soon as this little period of adjustment that you're going through right now passes over.

ISABEL. May I call my father, collect?

RALPH. Don't call home, now. Why upset the old people on Christmas Eve?

ISABEL. I'll just say I miss them and want to come home for Christmas.

RALPH. They'll know something's wrong if you go home without your brand-new husband.

ISABEL. Husband! What husband? That man who refers to me as

35

a Tokyo whore? Implies that I seduced him in a hospital because I was required to give him alcohol rub-downs at bedtime?

RALPH. All he meant was you excited him, honey.

ISABEL. I assure you that was *not* my intention! I am naturally gentle, I am gentle by nature, and if my touch on his big lecherous body created—*sexual (George re-enters, turns out bathroom light —puts bag on bed then crosses c.) fantasies* in his *mind!*—that's hardly *my* fault, is it?

GEORGE. (*Returning.*) I'm sorry that I upset you.

ISABEL. Will you tell him the truth?

GEORGE. (*At chair L.*) Sure I will. What about?

ISABEL. Did I deliberately excite you in Barnes Hospital?

GEORGE. No. I never said that.

ISABEL. Anybody that heard you would get that impression.

GEORGE. You didn't deliberately do it, you just did it because I was horny for you, that's all, that's all, that's—all . . . (*Turns away. He slumps in a chair with a long, despairing sigh. Pause— Silence. Ralph crosses u. to bar, then Isabel crosses to R. of George.*)

ISABEL. (*Softly.*) George, I don't blame you alone. I blame myself, too. Not for deliberate sexual provocation, but for not realizing before our marriage yesterday that we are (*She looks down.*) —opposite types.

GEORGE. (*Pause, he looks at her, then away—sadly.*) Yes, opposite types . . .

ISABEL. (*To Ralph.*) *I want to call my father!*

GEORGE. (*Crossing to bar.*) Talk to him. Call him. I'll pay Ralph the charges.

ISABEL. (*To Ralph.*) May I?

RALPH. Sure, honey, call home and wish 'em a Merry Christmas.

ISABEL. (*Crosses to chair, sits, dials "O."*) Thank you.—I will if I can stop crying.

RALPH. (*Crossing around to front of her.*) George? This little girl needs you. Go on, be nice to her, boy.

GEORGE. I need somebody, too. She hasn't got the incurable shakes, *I* have, *I* got 'em! Was *she* nice to *me? Last night?*

ISABEL. (*Tearfully.*) Hello, Operator? I want to call long distance, Sweetwater, Texas. Oh-seven-oh-three. No, anybody who answers. (*To them.*) It will be Daddy, Mama can't get out of —— (*Sob.*)

36

—bed! (*Ralph makes a sign to George to go over and sit by her. George disregards the suggestion.*)

RALPH. (*Crosses C.*) You better hang up and let them call you back. Long distance is very busy on Christmas Eve. Everyone callin' the home-folks. (*George moves to onstage stool.*)

ISABEL. I just hope I stop crying! I don't want Daddy to hear me. (*Pause.*) Poor ole thing. So sweet and faithful to Mama, bedridden with arthritis for seven years, now. (*George crosses to sofa, sits.*) . . . Hello? What? Oh. You'll call me right back as soon as you make the connection, will you, because it's very important, (*Ralph crosses to phone, points to number on dial.*) it's really very urgent . . . this number is High Point 7268. (*Hangs up. Silence.*)

RALPH. (*Ralph looks at her, no reaction, then crosses to George, no reaction then sits on stool C. Finally.*) One bad night in a rutten highway motel and you all are acting like born enemies toward each other!

GEORGE. Don't upset her, she's going to talk to her daddy. And tell him she's married to a stinker.

ISABEL. No, I'm not. I'm going to tell him that I am blissfully happy, married to the kindest man in the world, the second kindest, the kindest man next to my daddy!

GEORGE. Thanks.

ISABEL. Waits hand and foot on Mama, bedridden with arthritis.

GEORGE. You told Ralph about that.

ISABEL. And has held down a job in a pharmacy all these years . . .

GEORGE. Wonderful.

ISABEL. You see, I was spoiled as a girl because I had such a father, he set me too high a standard for the men I met since . . .

GEORGE. I didn't expect to marry a girl in love with her father.

ISABEL. George Haverstick, you are truly a monster! (*Phone rings. [Sound No. 15] Isabel, snatching it up.*) What?—DAD! OH, PRECIOUS DADDY! (*Bursts into violent tears.*) Can't talk, can't talk, can't talk, can't talk, can't—talk! (*Raises phone.*)

RALPH. (*Crossing to above her, takes phone, offers it to George. George turns D. Ralph then talks.*) Honey, gi' me the phone! Hello? Hi, Pop, merry Christmas. No, this isn't George, this is a buddy of his. Isabel wants to talk to you to tell you how happy she is, but she just broke up with emotion. You know how it is, don't you, Pop? Newlyweds? They're naturally full of emotion.

37

They got to go through a little adjustment period between them. —Fine, yes, she's fine. She'll talk to you soon as she blows her nose. Hey, honey? Your daddy wants to talk to you. (*She takes the phone, then bursts into violent sobbing again, covering her mouth and handing the phone back to Ralph.*) Pop? I'll have to talk for her. She's all shook up. (*He forces the phone back into Isabel's hand.*)

ISABEL. (*Choked.*) Dad? (*Bawls again, covering the mouthpiece. Ralph takes the phone back from her.*)

RALPH. Pop? Just talk to her, Pop. She's too shook up to talk back. (*Forces phone into her hands again.*)

ISABEL. Dad? How are you, Daddy? Are you? That's wonderful, Daddy. Oh, I'm fine, too. I got married yesterday. Yesterday. . . . How is Mom? Just the same?—Daddy? I may be seeing you soon. Yes. You know I gave up my nursing job at Barnes when I married and so I have lots of free time and I might just suddenly pop in on you—*tomorrow!*—I love you and miss you so much! Goodbye, Merry Christmas, Daddy! (*Hangs up blindly and crosses to Xmas tree. She looks at George as she crosses U.*) I think it's awful your little boy's missing his Christmas. Such a wonderful Christmas. A choo-choo train with depot and tunnel, cowboy outfit, chemical set and a set of alphabet blocks . . .

GEORGE. He knows what he got for his kid, you don't have to tell him. (*Pause. She turns D.*)

ISABEL. Well, now, I feel better, after talking to Daddy.

GEORGE. Does it make you feel uplifted, spiritually?

ISABEL. I feel less lonely. That's all.

GEORGE. I wonder if it would have that effect on me if I called my daddy or mama in Amarillo? That's in Texas, too. Maybe I'd feel less lonely. Huh, Little Bit? (*Dog enters from dinette, crosses D. C. Isabel takes dog by collar—kneels to pet it.*)

ISABEL. Such a sweet animal! Mr. Bates, would your animal like to go for a walk? What is this animal's name?

GEORGE. The animal is a dog.

ISABEL. I know it's a dog.

GEORGE. (*He crosses U. to bar.*) Then why don't you call it a dog!

RALPH. Better put 'er lead on 'er. Her name is Bessie.

ISABEL. Shall we take a walk, Bessie? Huh? A nice little run in

38

the snow? She said yes. Oh! my coat. . . (*She rises, crosses towards coat.*)

RALPH. (*He crosses* U. *to tree, gets coat box, sets it on stool* D. C., *pulls out coat.*) Here, put on this one, honey.

ISABEL. (*She crosses to* L. *of Ralph who is holding out coat.*) Oh, what a beautiful sheared beaver! It's your wife's Christmas present?

RALPH. It was but it ain't no more.

ISABEL. How soft! (*Strokes it.*) Now I know that you love her. You couldn't feel the softness of this fur and not know it was bought as a present for someone you love.

RALPH. (*Starts to put it on her.*) Put it on. It's yours. A wedding present to you.

ISABEL. (*Retreats toward door.*) Oh, no I ——

RALPH. (*Crossing* U. *to her, puts it around her.*) WILL YOU PLEASE PUT IT ON YUH?

ISABEL. I guess the snow won't hurt it. Come on, Bessie, that's a good lady, come on . . . (*She crosses out to porch.*)

GEORGE. (*Crossing* D. *to Ralph.*) I know of two animals that went out and one of them ain't no dawg!

ISABEL. (*She re-enters to doorway.*) I heard that!

GEORGE. (*Steps* C.) Well, good!

ISABEL. If you want out of our marriage, a divorce isn't necessary. We can just get an annulment! So maybe last night was fortunate after all! (*She exits* L.)

GEORGE. (*Closes door.*) How much money you got?

RALPH. Why?

GEORGE. (*Crossing towards Ralph.*) Remember how we talked about going into something together when we got out of the service? Well, we're out of the service. How much money do you think you can raise?

RALPH. What are *your* assets, Buddy?

GEORGE. I've saved five hundred dollars and can get a thousand for that '52 Caddy.

RALPH. (*Just* U. R. *of* C. *stool.*) You can't go into no business on as little as that.

GEORGE. You're selling out this house and everything in it, ain't you?

RALPH. I'd have to split it with Dorothea, I reckon. I don't know

39

what I'll be able to get for it. This place is built right over a cavern.

GEORGE. What?

RALPH. Yeah! This whole High Point suburb is built right over a subterranean cavern and is gradually sinking into it inch by inch by year.

GEORGE. What are you talking about?

RALPH. You notice the cracks on the walls? (*George crosses to front door.*) Of course it isn't publicly known. The property owners have gotten together to keep it a secret until we've sold out, in alphabetical order— (*George crosses from door to L. of sofa.*) at a loss, but not a complete sacrifice. (*George starts to say something.*) I know. Collusion, connivance. Disgusting but necessary.

GEORGE. (*Leaning over sofa.*) Look. Let's cut out tomorrow. Let's go to Texas together. We can swing the financing to pick up a piece of ranchland near San Antone and raise us a herd of fine cattle.

RALPH. Why San Antone?

GEORGE. I said near it. It's a beautiful town. A winding river goes through it.

RALPH. Uh-huh. You mentioned "swing the financing." How did you—visualize—that?

GEORGE. Notice my car out there?

RALPH. That old funeral limousine?

GEORGE. (*Sits on u. arm of sofa.*) We cut out of here tomorrow bright and early and drive straight through to West Texas. In West Texas we git us a colored boy, put a showfer's cap on him an' set him back of the wheel. He drives us up in front of the biggest San Antone bank and there we demand an immediate interview with the president of it. My folks staked out West Texas. The name of the first George Haverstick in West Texas is engraved on the memorial tablet to the Alamo heroes in San Antone! I'm not snowin' you, man! An' they's no better credit card in West Texas than an ancestor's name on that memorial tablet. We will arrive at lunch-time and—invite this bank executive to lunch at the San Antone country club to which I can git us a guest-card an' befo' we're in sight of the golf-links the financing deal will be swung! (*Backs off L. 2 steps.*)

RALPH. Man, a bank president has rode in too many funeral

limousines not to know when he's in one. Driving in funeral processions is almost one of his main professional duties. (*He rises, crosses to George, pats his hands which are hidden in pockets.*) And ain't you afraid that he might, well—notice your shakes?

GEORGE. This little tremor would disappear completely the moment I crossed into Texas!

RALPH. (*Puts hand on George's shoulders.*) I hope so, man, permanently and completely, but ——

GEORGE. (*Shakes him off, crosses u. to bar.*) BUT, YEAH BUT! Go on. Tear down the project!

RALPH. (*Crossing D. to TV.*) There's no Ralph Bates, first, second, third, fourth or fifth on that memorial tablet to those— (*Turns on TV. We hear "Jingle Bells."*) [Sound No. 16] Alamo heroes.

GEORGE. (*Crosses D. to Ralph, with beer.*) Haven't you blazoned your name in the memory of two wars?

RALPH. Who remembers two wars? Or even one, after some years. There's a great public amnesia about a former war hero. (*Ralph crosses to front door, goes to porch.*)

GEORGE. (*Follows to C.*) Where you goin'?

RALPH. (*Turns on Xmas lights, crosses D. on porch. George closes door, crosses D. to L. of Ralph.*) I'm goin' out to think in this cool night air. Why San Antone? Why cattle? Why not electric equipment?

GEORGE. I know San Antone and cattle!

RALPH. And I know electric equipment.

GEORGE. Yes, you can turn on a set of little Christmas tree lights.

RALPH. (*Sits R. on stool D.*) I don't want to be your ranch hand!

GEORGE. We'd buy in EQUAL.

RALPH. Also ——

GEORGE. Also WHAT?

RALPH. Why cattle?

GEORGE. The Texas Long Horn is a dignified beast.

RALPH. Did you say Texas Long Horn? Son. The Texas Long Horn is not only dignified, it is *obsolete*.

GEORGE. Historical, yeah, like the Haversticks of West Texas.

RALPH. The Haversticks of West Texas are not yet obsolete, are they?

GEORGE. Well, I am the last one of them, and the prospects of

41

another don't look too bright at the moment. (*Sits* L. *of Ralph.*)
But the Texas Long Horn—compared to modern beef cattle such
as your Hereford or your Black Angus—it has no carcass value.

RALPH. Well, in that case, why don't you *breed* the Black Angus
or the ——

GEORGE. I anticipated that question.

RALPH. I hope you're prepared with some answer . . .

GEORGE. Let me put it this way. *You* got TV in there, ain't you?
Turn on your TV any late afternoon or early evenin' and what do
you get? A goddam Western, on film. Y' know what I see, outside
the camera range? A big painted sign that says: "Haverstick-Bates
Ranch"—"The Last Stand of the Texas Long Horn, a Dignified
Beast"!—*We breed cattle for TV Westerns*—We breed us some
buffalo, too. The buffalo is also a dignified beast, almost extinct,
only thirty thousand head of the buffalo left in this land. We'll
increase that number by a sizeable fraction. Hell, we could double
that number befo' we ——

RALPH. Hang up our boots an' saddles under the—dignified sky
of West Texas?

GEORGE. There IS dignity in that sky! There's dignity in the
agrarian, the pastoral—way of—existence! A dignity too long lost
out of the—American dream . . . as it used to be in the West
Texas—Haverstick days . . .

RALPH. But I want to be dignified, too.

GEORGE. Human dignity's what I'm talkin' about.

RALPH. I don't want to be caught short by a Texas Long Horn
while crossing a pasture one mawnin' in West Texas! Ha ha ha—
Naw, I don't want to catch me an ass full of Texas Long Horns
before I can jump a fence-rail *out* of that West Texas pasture.
I ——

GEORGE. (*Rises, crosses* U., *2 steps.*) SHUT UP! WILL YUH?
YOU TV WATCHIN', CANNED BEER DRINKIN', SPANISH
SUBURBAN STUCCO TYPE SON OF—— (*Crosses* D., *takes
beer can from Ralph.*) Y'KNOW I THINK BEER IS DOPED?
DOPED? I THINK THEY DOPE IT TO CREATE A
NATIONAL TOLERANCE OF THE TV COMMERCIAL.
(*Tosses can off* L.) —No.—No.—I'm sorry I come through Nash-
ville . . . I cherished a memory of you.—Idolized an old picture
of which I was suddenly faced with a, with a—*goddam travesty*
of it!—When you opened the door and I was confronted with a

—MIDDLE-AGED! NEGATIVE! DEFEATED! LOST!—poor—
bastard . . .

RALPH. (*Rises, crosses* u., *to* u. *rail, as George crosses* R. *on
porch.*) What do you think I saw when I opened that door?
(*Crossing* D.) A ghostly apparition!

GEORGE. ME?

RALPH. You! A young man I used to know with an old man's
affliction—the palsy! (*Crosses* u. *3 steps.*)

GEORGE. (*Sits on bench.*) —Thanks!—I appreciate that. Oh,
man, oh, brother, I sure do appreciate that! Yeah. In addition to
those other changes I mentioned in you, you've now exposed another which is the worst of the bunch. You've turned *vicious!*

RALPH. (*Crosses* D. *above George.*) Aw.

GEORGE. Yeah, yeah, bitter and vicious! To ridicule an affliction
like mine, like this, is *vicious!* (*Ralph puts hand on George's
shoulder. George throws it off.*) *Take that mother-grabbin' hand
off my shoulder or I'll break it off you!*

RALPH. (*To him.*) You ridiculed my affliction.

GEORGE. What affliction?

RALPH. (*Off* L.) My life has been an affliction. (*He says this
without self-pity: simply as a matter of fact.*) To live a life in a
Spanish type stucco cottage in a—high point over a cavern, that
is an affliction for someone that wanted and dreamed of—oh, *I
wish I could be the first man in a moon rocket!* No, not the moon,
but Mars, Venus! Hell, I'd like to be transported and transplanted
to colonize and fertilize to be the Adam on a—star in a different
galaxy—yeah, that far away even!—it's wonderful knowing that
such a thing is no longer inconceivable, huh?

GEORGE. You're talking out of character. You're a dedicated con-
formist, the most earthbound earth man on earth.

RALPH. If you think that about me, you never known me. (*Carol-
lers are heard singing God Rest Ye Merry Gentlemen. [Sound
No. 17] Ralph sits* u. *of George, puts hand on* R. *shoulder.*)

GEORGE. Keep your rutten hand off my shoulder.

RALPH. Break it off me. I'm sorry I ridiculed your affliction.

GEORGE. (*Pause: apology accepted.*) What I mean is, the point
is—you *chose* your afflictions! Married into them. Mine I didn't
choose!—It just come on me, mysteriously: my shakes. (*Rises,
crosses* u. L. *of Ralph.*) You wouldn't even be interested in the
awful implications of an affliction like mine.

43

RALPH. Sure, I'm interested in it!

GEORGE. (C. *porch*.) S'pose it never lets up? This thing they can't treat or even find the cause of! S'pose I shake all my life like, like —dice in a crap shooter's fist!?—Huh?—I mean at all moments of tension, all times of crisis, I shake!! . . . Huh?—And there's other aspects to it beside the career side . . . —It could affect my love life. Huh. I could start shaking so hard when I started to make out with a girl that I couldn't do it. You know? Couldn't make the scene with her . . . (*Slight pause*.)

RALPH. Aw. Was that it?

GEORGE. Was what what?

RALPH. Was that the trouble at the Old Man River Motel, last night, you were scared of impotence with her? Was that the problem?

GEORGE. —I don't have that problem. I never had that problem.

RALPH. No?

GEORGE. NO! (*Tense pause*.) WHY? Do *you* have that problem?

RALPH. Sometimes I wasn't excited enough by Dotty to satisfy her, sometimes . . . Poor ole Dotty. She's got so she always wants it and when I can't give it to her I feel guilty, guilty. . . . (*Rises crosses* U. *Turns Christmas lights off again, turns them back on again*.)

GEORGE. (*Front*.) Well, you know *me*. An Ever-ready Battery, built-in in me.

RALPH. (*Turning to him with a slow, gentle smile*.) Yeah, I understand, son.

GEORGE. Don't be so damned understanding! (*Starts to change into house, discovers door locked*.) Open this goddam door!

RALPH. (*Tries door*.) You shut the door and I had the catch on it, we'll have to climb in a window.

GEORGE. *You* climb in a window and lemme in this door.

RALPH. (*Crossing* D.) There she goes, Mrs. George Haverstick the Fifth, she's going up to the wrong Spanish type stucco cottage, there's five almost identical ones in this block. (*Whistles*.) You better go get her while I climb in a window. (*Exits through door to car-port*.)

GEORGE. (*Gloomily, to himself*.) I don't want her now, no more than she wants me. Hell, I wouldn't give it to her if she asked me for it, the way I feel. (*He crosses out through the carport. George*

44

is not inclined to be merry. He glares into the starless air. In the bedroom, Ralph gets the window up and clambers through with some muttered invectives against the hostility of the inanimate objects of the world. Soon as he enters the interior, light and sound inside are brought up. Oddly enough, a TV Western is in progress, approaching the climax of an Indian attack or a cattle stampede. [Sound No. 18] It catches Ralph's attention: he turns gravely to the TV set, for the moment forgetting George outside. Gun-fire subsides and dialogue is brought up loud.)

TV DIALOGUE. —What is our chances, you think?—You want a *honest* answer or a *comforting* answer?—Give me the honest answer.—The comforting answer would have been fifty-fifty: I'll leave you to imagine the honest answer. *(Ralph, starting for front door, stops to look.)* —Rosemary? Yes, Buck. Come here, a minute. Take this pistol. There's five shots in it. Save the fifth shot for yourself. Now git on this hawss behind me.—Oh, Buck! I'm so scared! *(Ralph pulls stool front of TV.)* —Git up!—OK, sweetheart?—Yes!—Hold onto me tight.

GEORGE. Motherless bastard!

TV DIALOGUE. *(Continuing.)* Dusty, when I count ten, start the cattle stampede. *(He starts counting slowly.)*

GEORGE. BATES! REMEMBER ME? Jesus!

RALPH. *(Crosses to door, lets George in: sits on stool.)* I thought you'd gone for your wife.

GEORGE. *(Crosses to L. of Ralph.)* See what I mean? A western on Christmas Eve even, it's a national obsession. And will you look at those miserable short-horn *cows?*

RALPH. Yep. Undignified beasts. Man? Buddy, I don't have too much confidence in the dignified long-horn project, but I will go along with you:—Don't ask me why: *(Crosses u. c. with George.)* I couldn't tell you why: But I will go along with you. —Want to shake on it, Buddy?

GEORGE. *(Dragging him out to dinette.)* Break out the champagne, it ought to be cold by now.

RALPH. *(Stopping.)* It'll be colder when you've picked up your wife.

GEORGE. Pick up your own wife. Leave mine alone. *(Isabel enters L.)* That champagne ought to be colder than a well digger's ass in Wyoming. *(They exit to dinette.)*

RALPH. Or a nun's knee in, Siberia.

GEORGE. What do you hear from One-Eye Reilly?
      As I was sitting on Reilly's doorstep
      listening to the tales of blood and slaughter
      came a thought into my mind
      why not shag old Reilly's daughter
      Fiddley I ee
      Fiddley I O
      Fiddley I ee for the
      Fiddley I one-eyed Reilly
      Rig-a-dig-jig eyes and all

(Isabel enters and unleashes the cocker spaniel as the men burst into a barracks-room song, very loud and vulgar. Isabel is revolted by a particularly lewd phrase. She rushes into the bedroom for bag, but sees and snatches up the Infant.)

ISABEL. *(Sits front of* D. *bed.)* Oh little boy Jesus, so lonesome on your birthday. I know just how you feel. I feel the same way too.

CURTAIN

ACT III

No time lapse.

Men return with open, foaming bottle of champagne, and two glasses, not noticing that dog has returned, or suspecting Isabel's presence in the bedroom. [Sound No. 19 is still on] George crosses L. to chair, sits. Ralph crosses D. to TV, turns it off, then sits on sofa. Isabel same position as close of act II.)

GEORGE. I put women in five categories. Those that worship it, those that love it, those that just like it, those that don't like it, those that just tolerate it, those that *don't* tolerate it, those that can't stand it, and, finally, those that not only can't stand it but want to cut it off you.

RALPH. (*Rises, crosses to TV, gets bottle, pauses.*) That's more than five categories.

GEORGE. How many did I name?

RALPH. (*Crosses back to sofa, sits.*) I don't know. I lost count.

GEORGE. Well, you know what I mean. And I have married into that last category. What scares me is that she has had hospital training and is probably able to do a pretty good cutting job. (*Isabel rises, crosses U. to listen at bedroom door.*)

RALPH. Ha ha, yeah. Wel-l-l. (*Sets glasses down and takes the bottle from George in the little parlor, flickering with firelight.*)

GEORGE. Which class did you marry into? Into the last category?

RALPH. No. She got to like it. More than I did even.

GEORGE. Now you're braggin'.

RALPH. (*Crosses to stool, sits.*) Love is a very difficult—occupation. You got to work at it, man. It ain't a thing every Tom, Dick and Harry has got a true aptitude for. Y'know what I mean? Not every Tom, Dick or Harry understands how to use it. It's not a—offensive weapon. It shouldn't be used like one. Too many guys, they use it like a offensive weapon to beat down a woman with.

47

All right. That rouses resistance. Because a woman has pride, even a woman has pride (*Isabel sits on bed* u.) and resents being raped and most love-making is rape with these self-regarded—experts! That come downstairs yelling, "Oh, man, oh, brother," and hitching their belts up like they'd accomplished something.

GEORGE. (*Rises. Getting the allusion and resentful.*) —You mean me?

RALPH. Naw, naw, will yuh listen a minute? I've got ideas on this subject.

GEORGE. (*Sits.*) Sure—a self-regarded expert!

RALPH. You know goddam right I'm an expert. I know I never had your good looks but made out better.

GEORGE. That's one man's opinion!

RALPH. Look! Lissen! You got to use—TENDERNESS!—with it, not roughness, snatch-and-grab roughness but true tenderness with it or ——

GEORGE. O.K., build yourself up! If that's what you need to!

RALPH. Naw, now, lissen! You know I know what I'm sayin'!

GEORGE. Sure, self-regarded expert! (*They are both pretty high now.*)

RALPH. I know what went wrong last night at that Cape Girardeau motel as well as if I had seen it all on TV!

GEORGE. What went wrong is that I found myself hitched up with a woman in the "cut-it-off" category! (*Isabel is listening to all this in the bedroom. She stands up and sits down, stands up and sits down, barely able to keep from shouting something.*)

RALPH. Aw, naw, aw, naw. I will tell you what happened. What happened, man, is this! You didn't appreciate the natural need for using some tenderness with it. Lacking confidence with it, you wanted to hit her, smash her, (*George crosses to sofa, pours drink, sits.*) clober her with it. You got violence in you. That's what made you such a good fighter pilot, the best there was! Sexual violence, that's what gives you the shakes, (*George crosses* u. *then to door.*) that's what makes you unstable. That's what made you just sit on the straw mats with the Tokyo dolls, drinking sake with them, teaching them English till it was time to come downstairs and holler, "Oh, man, oh, brother" like you had them laid to waste! (*Slight pause. George is sweating, flushed.*)

GEORGE. (*Turns to Ralph.*) Where did you ever hear a story like that?

48

RALPH. I heard it directly from them, you just sat up there drinkin' sake with 'em an' teachin' 'em English, and then you'd come down shouting, "Oh, man, oh, brother!" like you had laid 'em to waste.

GEORGE. (*Crosses to Ralph's* L.) Which of them told you this story?

RALPH. *Which* of them? ALL! EV'RY ONE! (*Pause. Isabel sits down on the bed again, raises her hands to either side of her face, slowly shaking her head with a gradual comprehension.*)

GEORGE. (*Threatens, then turns away.*) Man, at this moment I'd like to bust your face in!

RALPH. I'm tryin' to help you. Don't you know that I am tryin' t' help you? (*Pause. They look away from each other in solemn reverie for some moments. Isabel rises again from the bed but still doesn't move. After some moments she sits back down. She is crying now. Ralph, continuing gently:*) You have got this problem.

GEORGE. (*Crossing to Ralph, explaining lightly.*) In Tokyo I never told you ——

RALPH. What?

GEORGE. I had a girl on the side. I mean a nice one. I was choosy. One that I wanted to keep to myself, strictly. I didn't want to expose her to a bunch of ——

RALPH. Aw, now, man, you don't have to start fabricating some kind of a Sayonara fantasy like this!

GEORGE. (*Attacking again.*) How about Big Springs, Texas?

RALPH. What about Big Springs, Texas, besides being boring, I mean, what *else* about it?

GEORGE. Plenty. I fixed you up there. You never got nowhere in Big Springs, Texas till I opened it up for you.

RALPH. (*Puts hand on George's shoulder.*) Baby, don't be sore.

GEORGE. (*Shakes off Ralph's hand.*) Sore, I'm not sore. You've done your damndest to make me feel like a phoney, but I'm not sore. *You're* sore. Not *me. I'm* not sore.

RALPH. You sure are shaking.

GEORGE. Yeah, well, I got this tremor . . . Jesus, my goddam voice is got the shakes too! But you know it's the truth, in Big Springs, Texas we had the best damn time you ever had in your life, and I broke the ice, there, for you.

RALPH. I don't deny that women naturally like you. Everybody likes you! Don't you know that? People never low-rate you! Don't you know that? I like you. That's for sure. But I hate to see you shaking because of ——

GEORGE. (*Cutting in.*) Look! We're both free, now. Like two birds. You're gonna cut out of this High Point Over a Cavern. And we'll buy us a piece of ranch-land near San Antone and ——

RALPH. Yeah, yeah, let's go back to what we wuh tawkin' about. *Tenderness.* With a *woman*.

GEORGE. I don't want to hear a goddam lecture from you about such a thing as that when here you are, night before Christmas, with just (*Points* U.) a cocker spaniel and presents under a tree, with no one to *take* them from you!

RALPH. (*Abruptly. Rising.*) *Hey!*

GEORGE. *Huh?*

RALPH. (*Crosses* U. *to dog. George counters* C.) Th' dawg is back. How *come?!*

GEORGE. (*At* C.) The dawg come back, tha's all . . . (*Isabel comes out of the bedroom carrying beaver coat. Ralph crosses to door, opens it, tries latch. Then, as Isabel enters, George sees her, hits Ralph, who turns in.*)

ISABEL. Yes, I brought the dog back. (*Folds coat and puts it in box on table. Pause, rather long.*)

RALPH. We, uh, we—saw you going up to the wrong—Spanish-type cottage . . .

ISABEL. I haven't discovered the *right* one, Mr. Bates.

RALPH. I ain't discovered it either.

GEORGE. What kept you so long in the wrong one?

ISABEL. They invited me in to a lovely buffet supper while they looked up the High Point Bates in the phone-book. (*Pause. She crosses* C. *to tree, sets box under it.*) I heard your very enlightening conversation from the bedroom. (*George crosses* D. *to TV, sets bottle, crosses* U. *to bar, Ralph kicks dog off stool, crosses to George, she steps down then crosses* L., *gets coat, puts it on, crosses* R., *picks up blue bag, crosses* C., *turns the them.*) You're a pair of small boys. Boasting, bragging, showing off to each other. . . . I want to call a cab. I'm going downtown, Gawge. (*He crosses unsteadily to phone, lifts it and hands it to her with an effort at stateliness.*)

GEORGE. (*Steps in.*) Whacha want, yellow checkered or what? I'll git it for yuh! (*She crosses to phone.*)

RALPH. (*Crosses above her, to stop her.*) Put down th' phone. (*Isabel dials Operator.*)

GEORGE. (*Steps to C.*) Leave her alone. Let her go downtown. She's free to. (*Ralph takes the phone from her and puts it back in the cradle.*)

ISABEL. (*Crossing U., between them.*) Do I have to walk? (*Crosses to door, opens it and starts out. A car is heard stopping.*) [*Sound No. 20*] There's a car in front of your house, Mr. Bates.

RALPH. (*Crosses above her to rail.*) YEP! IT'S HER OLD MAN'S CAR! Dorothea's papa, my ex-boss!

ISABEL. Perhaps he'll be kind enough to—take me downtown.

RALPH. (*Escorts her in towards bedroom.*) Get back in, little lady! Stay in the bedroom till I git through this! Then I'll drive you downtown if you're still determined to go. (*Passing George.*) SET DOWN, GAWGE! For Chrissakes. Little lady, will you please wait in the bedroom till I get through this hassle with her old man?

ISABEL. (*At bedroom.*) Yes, all right, I will, but please don't forget your promise to take me downtown right afterwards. (*She returns to bedroom with dignity. Mr. and Mrs. McGillicuddy appear before the house. They cross onto porch, he is by door. They are a pair of old bulls.*)

MRS. McGILLICUDDY. The first thing to discuss is their joint savings account. I wish you'd listened to me an' brought your lawyer.

MR. McGILLICUDDY. I can handle that boy. You keep your mouth out of it. Just collect the silver and china and let me handle the talk. (*He knocks, dislodging Christmas wreath attached to the knocker. Mrs. McGillicuddy picks it up.*) Now what are you gonna do with that Christmas wreath? You gonna crown him with it? (*Knocks violently: Ralph starts up, then sits again. Ralph slowly crosses to door, indicating to George to remain seated. Ralph opens door.*)

RALPH. Well, Mr. and Mrs. *MAC!*

MR. McGILLICUDDY. (*Throwing wreath.*) This come off your knocker.

RALPH. Ha, ha, what a surprise!

MRS. McGILLICUDDY. We've come to pick up some things of Dorothea's.

51

RALPH. That's O.K. Take out anything that's hers, but don't touch nothing that belongs to us both. (*Susie enters* L. *to porch.*)

MRS. McGILLICUDDY. (*Crossing in to bar gather stuff.*) We've come with a list of things that belong exclusively to Dorothea!

MR. McGILLICUDDY. (*To Susie on porch.*) Well, Susie, you better tote the basket of my daughter's china down the terrace. Don't try to make the slippery front steps with it. (*Susie crosses to china by fire, sits.*)

RALPH. She's not takin' no china out of this house.

MR. McGILLICUDDY. (*Enters, crosses to sofa, sees George, drops hat on sofa.*) You're not going to sell a goddam thing of my daughter's in this house.

RALPH. (*Turns down to him.*) All I done was to call up Emory Sparks ——

MR. McGILLICUDDY (*Stopping him.*) Now hold on a minute, war hero!

RALPH. I don't like the way you always call me war hero!

MR. McGILLICUDDY. *Why?* Ain't that what you *were?*

GEORGE. (*Rises, crosses* U. *to* R. *of Mr. McGillicuddy.*) You're goddam right he was! I flown over seventy bombing missions with this boy in Korea and before that in the—Second World War.

MR. McGILLICUDDY. Yes, yes, yes, I know it backwards and forwards, and I know who you are. You are Haverstick, ain't you?

GEORGE. (*Crossing to bar.*) Yeah, you got the name right.

MR. McGILLICUDDY. Well, Haverstick, the war's over and you two bombers are grounded. Now, Susie, go in the kitchen and get that Mixmaster and that new Rotisserie out in the basket while I collect the silver in that sideboard in there. (*Susie rises, steps* D.)

RALPH. Susie, don't you go in my kitchen. You want to be arrested for trespassing, Susie?

SUSIE. No, sir!

MRS. McGILLICUDDY. (*Crosses* D. *to* TV, *takes ashtray.*) Stuart, you'd better call that policeman in here.

RALPH. NO! KIDDING!

MRS. McGILLICUDDY. (*Crosses to phone table, takes ashtray.*) We anticipated that you'd make trouble.

RALPH. How does Dorothea feel about you all doing this?

MR. McGILLICUDDY. (*Crossing to door. At door.*) OFFICER! ——

RALPH. (*Officer enters to porch.*) How does Dotty feel? What is her attitude toward this kind of —— (*Mrs. McGillicuddy crosses to bar. Ralph is trembling. His voice chokes. George rises and puts a hand on Ralph's shoulder as a young police officer enters looking embarrassed.*)

MR. McGILLICUDDY. You know the situation, Lieutenant. (*Ralph crosses out to R. of Mr. McGillicuddy.*) We have to remove my daughter's valuables from the house because we've been tipped off this man here, Ralph Bates, is intending to make a quick cash sale of everything in the house and skip out of Nashville tomorrow.

RALPH. THAT'S A GODDAM LIE! WHO TOLD YOU THAT?

MRS. McGILLICUDDY. (*She steps c. Ralph crosses into living room.*) Emory Sparks' fiancée is Dorothea's good friend! That's how we got that warning! She called to enquire if Dorothea was serious about this matter. How did Dotty feel, how did she FEEL? I'll tell you! SICK AT HER STOMACH! VIOLENTLY SICK AT HER STOMACH.

RALPH. (*Cuts her.*) I should think so, goddam it. I should THINK so! She's got many a fault she got from you two, but, hell, she'd no more agree to a piece of cheapness like this —— (*Crosses D. to TV.*)

MR. McGILLICUDDY. (*Crosses into living room c. Officer crosses into house, closes door, stands by it.*) How could there be any possible doubt about it when Emory Sparks' fiancée ——

RALPH. (*Crossing up to R. of Mr. McGillicuddy.*) Will you allow me to speak? I did call Emory Sparks and told him my wife had quit me because I had quit my job, and I merely suggested that he come over and look over the stuff here and see if any of all this goddam electric equipment and so forth would be of any use to him since it isn't to me and since I got to have some financial —— (*He becomes suddenly speechless and breathless. George embraces his shoulder.*)

GEORGE. Now, now, don't blow a gasket over it, son, this is going to work out.

RALPH. I think you folks had better consider some legal angles in what you're up to here.

MR. McGILLICUDDY. (*Puffing, red in face.*) Aw, there's no legal angle about it that I don't know, and if there was, I could cope with that, too.

MRS. McGILLICUDDY. (*Crossing toward bedroom from bar after giving bar stuff to Susie.*) That too!

MR. McGILLICUDDY. You got no goddam position in this town but what I give you!

RALPH. *Oh!* Uh-huh —— (*Mrs. McGillicuddy has crossed to bedroom and discovered Isabel in it.*)

MRS. McGILLICUDDY. *Stuart, they have a woman in Dotty's bedroom!*

RALPH. George's wife is in there.

MRS. McGILLICUDDY. (*Steps to him.*) How long have you been planning this? (*Knocks on bedroom door.*) Can I come in?

ISABEL. (*Rises.*) Please do. (*Mrs. McGilluddy enters bedroom.*)

MRS. McGILLICUDDY. (*Crossing towards dresser without looking at Isabel. Coldly.*) I've come to pick up some things that belong to my daughter. Susie! (*Ralph crosses to phone, gets glass, crosses to bar, sits onstage stool.*)

ISABEL. I told my husband we'd dropped in at the wrong moment.

MRS. McGILLICUDDY. (*Turning to her.*) May I ask who you are?

ISABEL. I'm Mrs. George Haverstick. You probably saw my husband in the front room.

MRS. McGILLICUDDY. Your husband's an old friend of Ralph's, one of his war-time buddies?

ISABEL. Yes, he is, Mrs. —I didn't get your name.

MRS. McGILLICUDDY. All I can say is "Watch out," if he's an old friend of Ralph's! (*Crosses to dresser.*)

ISABEL. Why?

MRS. McGILLICUDDY. (*Turns back.*) Birds of a feather, that's all. (*Mrs. McGillicuddy opens drawers and starts piling clothes on bed. In the living room, Mr. McGillicuddy takes a seat in silence on chair L.*)

ISABEL. (*In bedroom.*) Are you sure you're doing the right thing?

MRS. McGILLICUDY. (*Calling out door.*) Susie!

SUSIE. (*Crosses D. to bedroom, crosses to between beds.*) Yes, ma'am?

MRS. McGILLICUDDY. Take these clothes of Miss Dotty's out to the car. (*Susie carries out clothes.*)

ISABEL. I think young people should be given a chance to work things out by themselves.

MRS. McGILLICUDDY. You have no idea at all of the situation.

54

And I'm sure you have your own problems if you have married a friend of my daughter's husband. Is he living on his war record like Ralph Bates is?

ISABEL. (*With rising indignation.*) He has a distinguished war record and a nervous disability that was a result of seventy-two flying missions in Korea and, and—more than twice that many in —World War II.

MRS. McGILLICUDDY. *I'm sick of hearing about past glories! Susie! (Isabel crosses* U. *to Ralph at bar. Susie comes in again.*) When you come back, pick up all Dotty's shoes on the floor of that dressing room, put 'em in the bottom of the basket, you hear? Put some paper over them, and then pile her little undies on top of the paper. You hear?—Then! If you still have room in the basket, collect some of the china out of the sideboard and cupboards. Be very careful with that.

SUSIE. (*Crossing out to door.*) Yes'm.

MRS. McGILLICUDDY. Don't try to carry too much at one time, Susie.

SUSIE. Yes'm.

MRS. McGILLICUDDY. That walk and those steps are a hazard. You hear? (*Susie exits* L. *There had been a prolonged silence in the front room during the scene above which they have been listening to.*)

MR. McGILLICUDDY. (*At last, holding bottle.*) Well, you seem to be living the life of Riley. French champagne. And the woman in Dotty's bedroom, was she French too?

GEORGE. (*Steps in.*) That woman is my wife and if you, Jesus, (*To Ralph.*) If he wasn't your father in law. (*Isabel exits to bathroom.*)

MR. McGILLICUDDY. Her being your wife or ——

RALPH. (*Crossing* C.) She's Haverstick's wife and this boy has make a good marriage.

MR. McGILLICUDDY. That means as much to me as ——

RALPH. (*Takes bottle from him.*) There's no reason why it should mean —— (*Sits stool.*) I just answered your question.

MR. McGILLICUDDY. Why do you feel so rutten superior to me?

RALPH. Aw. Did you notice that?

MR. McGILLICUDDY. From the first time I met you. You have

55

always acted very superior to me for some unknown reason. I'd like to know what it is.

RALPH. Can I consider that question? For a minute?

MR. McGILLICUDDY. Yeah, consider it, will you?!—I fail to see anything *special* about you, war hero!

GEORGE. (*Crosses to Mr. McGillicuddy.*) Let me answer for him. He feels superior to you because you're a big fat male cow. (*Exits to dinette.*)

RALPH. Shut up, George. Well, Mr. Mac? (*Mrs. McGillicuddy re-enters to* R. C. *of living room.*) Let me ask you a question. Why did you ask me to marry your daughter? (*Stops Mrs. McGillicuddy.*)

MR. McGILLICUDDY. (*Rises.*) DID *WHAT?*

RALPH. ASK ME TO marry your daughter.

MR. McGILLICUDDY. I NEVER! Done any such thing and ——

RALPH. You mean to say you've forgotten that you suggested to me that I marry Dotty? (*Mrs. McGillicuddy crosses* U. R. *of tree, collects things.*)

MR. McGILLICUDDY. (*Advancing on Ralph.*) I never forgotten a thing in my adult life, but I never recollect any such recollections as that. I do remember a conversation I held with you soon after you started to work at Regal Dairy Products an' come to my office to quit because you said you weren't gittin' paid well enough an' th' work was monotonous to you.

RALPH. That's right. Five years ago this winter.

MR. McGILICUDDY. (*Ralph crosses to sofa, sets bottle, glass on table.*) I gave you a fatherly talk. I told you monotony was a part of life. And I said I had an eye on you, which I did at that time.

RALPH. (*Turns on Mr. McGillicuddy.*) How about the rest of the conversation? In which you said that Dotty was your only child, that you had no son, and Dotty was int'rested in me and if Dotty got married her husband would be the heir to your throne as owner of Regal Dairy Products an' its subsidiaries such as Royal Ice Cream and Monarch Cheese, huh?

MRS. McGILLICUDDY. HANH!

RALPH. An' you hadn't long for this world because of acute diabetes and so forth and ——

MRS. McGILLICUDDY. HANH!

RALPH. And I would be shot right into your shoes when you departed this world? Well, you sure in hell lingered! (*Sits on sofa.*)

MRS. McGILLICUDDY. (*Crossing* D.) ARE YOU GOING TO
SIT THERE LISTENING TO THIS, STUART? I'M NOT!
MR. McGILLICUDDY. Be still, Mama. I can talk for myself. (*She
counters* L.) I did discuss these things with you but how in the
hell did you arrive at the idea I asked you to marry my daughter?
MRS. McGILLICUDDY. HANH! (*George crosses to look out the
window as if the scene had ceased to amuse him.*)
RALPH. What other way could it be interpreted, Mac? (*He is no
longer angry.*)
MR. McGILLICUDDY. I offered you a splendid chance in the
world which you spit on by your disrespect, your superior ——!
RALPH. (*Rises to him.*) I respect Dorothea. Always did and still
do!
MR. McGILLICUDDY. I'm talkin' about your attitude to me!
RALPH. I know you are. That's all that you care about, not about
Dorothea. You don't love Dotty. She let you down by having psy-
chological problems that you brought on her, that you an' Mrs.
Mac gave her by pushing her socially past her social endowments.
MRS. McGILLICUDDY. WHAT DO YOU MEAN BY THAT?
RALPH. (*Crossing between them.*) Dotty was never cut out to
boost your social position in this city. Which you expected her to.
You made her feel inferior all her life.
MRS. McGILLICUDDY. *Me? Me?*
RALPH. Both of yuh. I respected her, though, and sincerely liked
her and I married Dotty. (*Crosses to chair, sits.*) Give me credit
for that, and provided her with an—offspring. Maybe not much
of an offspring, but an offspring, a male one, at least it started a
male one. I can't help it if she's turnin' him into a sissy, I ——
MRS. McGILLICUDDY. MY GOD, STUART, HOW LONG
ARE YOU GONNA STAND THERE AND LISTEN TO THIS
WITHOUT ——
MR. McGILLICUDDY. *Mama, I told you to keep your mouth
outa this!*
RALPH. Yeah, but I MARRIED your baby! Give me credit for
that. And provided her with an—offspring!
MRS. McGILLICUDDY. What does he mean by that? That *he*
had the baby, not Dotty?
MR. McGILLICUDDY. Mama, I told you to keep your mouth
out of this!!!

MRS. McGILLICUDDY. He talks like he thought he did Dotty a FAVOR!

RALPH. (*Rises, crosses to them.*) Now, listen. I put up a five-year battle between our marriage and your goddam hold on her! You wouldn't release her though I doubt you always wanted her unmarried.

MRS. McGILLICUDDY. (*Crosses u. then counters L.*) OH, my —GOD!

MR. McGILLICUDDY. A bum like you?

RALPH. (*Advances threateneingly.*) Don't call me a bum.

MR. McGILLICUDDY. What in hell else *are* you? (*Retreats D. of stool.*) I give you your job which you quit today without warning!

RALPH. Wait! Like I said. I still respect your daughter, don't want to say anything not kind about her, but let's face facts. Who else but a sucker like me, Ralph Bates, would have married a girl with no looks, a plain, homely girl that probably no one but me had ever felt anything but just—SORRY FOR! —— (*Crosses u.*)

MRS. McGILLICUDDY. (*Crossing D. to Mr. McGillicuddy.*) OH GOD STUART! ARE YOU GOING TO STAND THERE AND LET HIM GO ON WITH THAT TALK?

RALPH. (*Crossing D. to L. of her.*) HOW IN HELL· DO YOU FIGURE HE'S GOING TO STOP ME?

MRS. McGILLICUDDY. (*Around Ralph to cop.*) OFFICER! CAN'T YOU GET THIS MAN OUT OF HERE? (*George re-enters, crosses D. to sofa, sits, has silverware.*)

OFFICER. No, ma'am. I can't arrest him.

RALPH. ARREST ME FOR WHAT, MRS. MAC? (*Then crosses to bar.*)

GEORGE. That's right, arrest him for what?

MRS. McGILLICUDDY. (*Crossing C.*) Stuart? Take out the silver. I don't know where Susie is. We should have come here with your lawyer as well as this—remarkably!—incompetent!—policeman. (*Exits to Bathroom.*)

MR. McGILLICUDDY. (*Crosses R. 2 steps.*) Susie took out the silver.

GEORGE. Naw, she didn't. I got the goddam silver. I'm sitting on it! (*He sits on silver, rises and stuffs it under sofa-pillow, having been discomfited by the forks.*)

MR. McGILLICUDDY. (*Crossing to cop.*) I guess I'll have to call

58

the Chief of Police who's a lodge-brother of mine and get a little more police cooperation than we have gotten so far.

OFFICER. O.K., you do that, Mister.

MR. McGILLICUDDY. He'll call you to the phone and give you exact instructions.

OFFICER. OK. I'll call him myself. If he gives 'em, I'll take 'em. (*Mrs. McGillicuddy has charged back into the bedroom to collect more things.*)

RALPH. (*Crossing* D. *to* R. C.) Mr. McGillicuddy, you are the worst thing any person can be: mean-minded, small-hearted, and *CHEAP!* Outstandingly and notoriously cheap! It was almost two months before I could *kiss* Dorothea, sincerely, after meeting her father! That's no crap. It wasn't the homeliness that threw me, it was the association she had in my mind with *you!!* It wasn't till I found out she despised you as much as I did that I was able to make real love to Dotty.

MR. McGILLICUDDY. (*Crossing* C.) My daughter is crazy about me!

RALPH. (*Sits sofa.*) You're crazy if you *think* so! (*Mrs. McGillicuddy comes out of bedroom.*)

MRS. McGILLICUDDY. (*Crossing* U. *to tree.*) All right. All of Dotty's clothes have been taken out. I think we may as well leave now.

MR. McGILLICUDDY. How about the TV? Which I gave Dotty *last* Christmas?

RALPH. (*Crosses* U., *then crosses to door, opens it.*) You want the TV? O. K.! TV! Take the TV out of here!—an' git out with it!

MRS. McGILLICUDDY. (*Mr. McGillicuddy starts down for TV, as Mrs. McGillicuddy crosses* D. *to him.*) What is that under the tree? It looks like a new fur coat!

RALPH. (*Steps in.*) That's right. A seven hundred and forty-five dollar sheared beaver coat that I'd bought for Dotty for Christmas! —but which I have just now presented to Mrs. George Haverstick as her weddin' present.

MR. McGILLICUDDY. The hell you have! How did you git hold of seven hundred and ——

RALPH. From my savings account.

MR. McGILLICUDDY. That was a *joint* account!

59

MRS. McGILLICUDDY. STUART! TAKE THAT COAT! GO ON, PICK UP THAT COAT!

RALPH. By God, if he touches that coat, I'll smash him into next week, and I never hit an old man before in my life!

MRS. McGILLICUDDY. OFFICER! PICK UP THAT COAT!

RALPH. I'll hit any man that tries to pick up that coat!

OFFICER. (*Putting down phone which he has been talking into quietly.*) I talked to my chief. He gave me my instructions. He says not to take any action that might result in publicity because of Mr. Bates having been a very well-known war hero. (*George rises, hands Mr. McGillicuddy his hat, crosses u. to bar.*)

MR. McGILLICUDDY. Come on, Mama. I'll just have to refer this whole disgusting business to my lawyer tomorrow, put it all in his hands and get the necessary papers to protect our baby.

MRS. McGILLICUDDY. (*Crosses to porch.*) I just want to say one thing more! Ralph Bates, don't you think for a moment that you are going to escape financial responsibility for the support of your child! Now come on, Stuart!—Isn't it pitiful? All that little boy's Christmas under the tree?

MR. McGILLICUDDY. C'mon Mama. Let's go home. (*They exit L. Officer shuts door.*)

RALPH. (*Follows, opens door.*) Send him over tomorrow to pick it all up: that can go out of the house, the little boy's Christmas can go . . . (*Re-enters, closes door, crosses to pouf front of fire. Isabel enters from bedroom.*)

ISABEL. (*Crossing to his R. George above him.*) Mr. Bates! I don't believe that this is what your wife wanted. I'll also bet you that she is outside in that car and if you would just stick your head out the door and call her, she would come running in here. (*Dorothea comes onto paved terrace, knocks at the door. Ralph does not move. She knocks again, harder and longer. He rises, crosses to door, hesitates.*) George, let his wife in the house.

GEORGE. Let's just keep out of this. I reckon he knows what he's doing. (*Isabel moves up to bar wall. Car honks. [Sound No. 4] Mrs. McGillicuddy's voice:*)

MRS. McGILLICUDDY. (*Off.*) Dorothea! Come back! We'll get the police!

DOROTHEA. (*Calling at door.*) Ralph? Ralph? It's Dotty! I want the child's Christmas things!

RALPH. (*At c.*) HE'LL GET THEM HERE OR NOWHERE!
(*Ralph paces back and forth in living room during this exchange.*)
DOROTHEA. *I'm not going to leave here without the child's
Christmas things!*—Ralph.
RALPH. *Let him come here alone tomorrow morning.*
DOROTHEA. *You can't do that to a child.*—Ralph! (*Car honks
again, long and loud.*) [*Sound No. 21*]
RALPH. (*Shouting back.*) Put the kid in a taxi in the morning
and I'll let him in to collect his Christmas presents!
MRS. McGILLICUDDY. Dorothea! I will not let you humiliate
yourself like this! Come away from that door!
DOROTHEA. Mama, stay in the car! (*Ralph sits on sofa.*)
MRS. McGILLICUDDY. Your father won't wait any longer. He's
started the car. He's determined to get the police.
DOROTHEA. RALPH! (*She has removed door key from bag.*)
I'M COMING IN!
MRS. McGILLICUDDY. *Dotty, where is your pride!* (*Isabel, then
George exit to dinette. Dorothea enters and slams door, crossing
to u. c. Dorothea stares at Ralph. He gazes stubbornly at the
opposite wall.*)
DOROTHEA. (*Steps in 1 step.*) I could tell you'd been drinkin'
by your voice. Who are these people you've got staying in the
house?
RALPH. Talk about the police! I could get you all arrested for
illegal entry!
DOROTHEA. (*Steps in 1 step.*) This is your liquor speaking, not
you, Ralph.
RALPH. You have abandoned me. You got no right by law to
come back into this house and make insulting remarks about my
friends.
DOROTHEA. Ralph? Ralph?—I know I acted—impetuously this
mawnin' . . .
RALPH. (*Rises, crosses to her, then crosses u.*) Naw, I think you
made the correct decision. You realized that you had tied yourself
down to a square peg in a round hole that had now popped out of
the hole and consequently would be of no further use to you. You
were perfectly satisfied for me to remain at that rutten little desk
job, tyrannized over by inferior men, for as long as my—heart
kept beating. (*Ends up by door.*)

61

DOROTHEA. No, Ralph. I wasn't. MY aim for you was your aim. Independence! A business of your own!

RALPH. Not when you were *faced* with it.

DOROTHEA. You sprung it on me at the wrong moment, Ralph. (*She crosses* D. *by* TV.) Our savings account is at a very low ebb.

RALPH. (*Crosses* D. *to chair, sits.*) Our savings account is all gone, little woman. It went on Christmas, all of it.

DOROTHEA. (*Crossing to him.*) *Mama* says you—bought me a *fur coat* for Christmas.

RALPH. (*Crosses to fire, sweeps up.*) Yeah, she took a look at it. Enquired the price. Wanted to take it off with her.

DOROTHEA. You wouldn't have bought me such a beautiful coat if you didn't still care for me, Ralph.—You know that, don't you?

RALPH. (*Slams down broom, opposite her at* R. C.) I made a decision affecting my whole future life. I know it was a big step, but I had the courage to make it.

DOROTHEA. I've always admired your courage.

RALPH. Hah!—I break the news. You walked right out on me, Dotty, takin' my son that you've turned into a sissy. He won't want these boys' toys under that tree. (*Crosses to bar, sits.*) What he'll want is a doll and a—tea set.

DOROTHEA. (*Picks up rocket launcher.*) All of these things are a little too old for Ralph Junior but he'll be delighted with them just the same, Ralph. (*Sets launcher down. Takes off her cloth coat.*) I'm going to try on that wonderful-looking beaver.

RALPH. It's not going out of the house, off you or on you, Dotty.

DOROTHEA. (*Picks up coat.*) Oh, how lovely, how lovely! (*Puts it on, he looks at her, then crosses* D. *to sofa, sits.*) Ralph, it *does* prove you love me!

RALPH. It cleaned out our savings account.

DOROTHEA. (*Crosses* D. *to pouf, sits.*) Both of us have been guilty of impetuous actions. You must've been awfully lonely, inviting a pair of strangers to occupy our bedroom on Christmas Eve.

RALPH. George Haverstick is not any stranger to me. (*Rises, crosses* U. *to tree.*) We both of us died in two wars, repeatedly died in two wars and were buried in suburbs named High Point but his (*Crosses* D. C.) was—hypenated. H-i-hyphen-Point. Mine was spelled out but was built on a cavern for the daughter and grand-child of Mr. and Mrs. Stuart McGillicuddy. (*Crosses to her* R.)

Oh, I told him something which I should have told you five years ago, Dorothea. I married you without love. I married you for ——
DOROTHEA. Ralph? Please don't!
RALPH. I married you for your stingy-fisted old papa's promise to ——
DOROTHEA. *Ralphie! Don't! I know!*
RALPH. —to make me his Heir Apparent! Assurances, lies! Even broad hints that he would soon kick off!
DOROTHEA. (*Stops him by putting her hands over his mouth.*) Ralph? Don't you know I know that?
RALPH. (*Holds her hands in front of him.*) Why'd you accept it? If you ——
DOROTHEA. I was so —— (*Covers her face.*)
RALPH. (*Drops her hands, crosses R. 2 steps.*) Cut it out, have some pride!
DOROTHEA. I *do!*
RALPH. In *what?*
DOROTHEA. In *you!*
RALPH. Oh, for the love of —— In me? Why, I'm telling you I'm nothin' better'n a goddam —— (*Crosses u. to bar.*)
DOROTHEA. I know, don't tell me again. I always knew it.—I had my nose done over and my front teeth extracted to look better for you, Ralphie!
RALPH. (*Crosses L. to door.*) "Ralphie!"—*Shoot* . . .
DOROTHEA. I *did* improve my appearance, didn't I, Ralph? It was extremely painful.
RALPH. (*Crosses R.*) Don't claim you done it for me! Every woman wants to improve on nature any way that she can. (*Crosses D. to L. of her.*) Yes! Of course you look better! You think you've won a *argument?*
DOROTHEA. *Me?—What* argument? *No!*—I've come back *crawling!*—not even embarrassed to do so! (*Isabel enters from kitchenette with coffee.*) Oh!—Hello. I didn't know you were —— (*Ralph crosses to chair, sits.*)
ISABEL. Mrs. Bates. I'm Isabel Haverstick. I took the liberty of making some coffee in your sweet little kitchen. Mrs. Bates, can I give you some coffee?
DOROTHEA. Thanks, that's awfully sweet of you, Mrs. Haverstick. It's nice of you and your husband to drop in on Ralph, but the situation between Ralph and me has changed. I guess I don't

have to explain it. You see I've come home. We only have one
bedroom and Ralph and I have an awful lot to talk over.

ISABEL. (*Sets tray on bar, picks up bag.*) I understand perfectly.
George and I are going to go right downtown.

DOROTHEA. (*Softening.*) You don't have to do that. This sofa
lets out to a bed and it's actually more comfortable than the beds
in the bedroom. I know, because other times when we've had a
falling out, less serious than this time, I have—occupied it. (*With
a little, soft, sad, embarrassed laugh. To Ralph.*) Of course, I
usually call'd Ralph in before mawnin' . . .

ISABEL. Oh, but this is no time for strangers to be here with you!

DOROTHEA. (*Now really warming.*) You all stay here! I insist!
It's really not easy to get a hotel room downtown with so many
folks coming into town for Christmas.

ISABEL. Well, if you're sure, if you're absolutely certain our presence wouldn't be inconvenient at all?—I do love this room. The
fire is still burning bright!—and the Christmas tree is so—pretty.

DOROTHEA. I'll tell my mother and father, they're still outside
in the car, to drive home and then we'll all have coffee together!
(*She rushes out in her beaver coat.*)

ISABEL. (*Crossing to* R. *of Ralph. George re-enters from dinette
to above Ralph.*) I like her! She's really nice!

RALPH. She just came back for the coat.

ISABEL. I think she came back for you.

RALPH. She walked out on me this morning because I had liber-
ated myself from a slave's situation!—and she took the kid with
her.

ISABEL. (*Sits on stool* C.) You're just going through a—period of
adjustment.

RALPH. We've been married six years.

ISABEL. But all that time you've been under terrible strain, hating
what you were doing, and maybe taking it out on your wife, Ralph
Bates. (*Car door slams. Car starts and moves off. [Sound No. 22]
and No. 23] Dorothea returns. Turns off porch lights and Xmas
lights, enters to above Ralph. George crosses* R. C. *Isabel crosses*
U. C.)

DOROTHEA. All right. I sent them home, much against their ob-
jections. I just *slammed* the car-door on them.

RALPH. They comin' back with the police?

DOROTHEA. No. You know they were bluffing.

ISABEL. (*Steps* D. *to sofa.*) Mrs. Bates, I would like you to know my husband, George Haverstick. I think you two should have your coffee alone in your own little bedroom. We'll all get acquainted tomorrow.

DOROTHEA. (*Crosses to bar, picks up tray with coffee, crosses to bedroom, sets tray on night table, then crosses to dressing table. Isabel crosses* L. C.) Ralph?

RALPH. (*Crosses to* R. C. *Sadly.*) I don't know.—We're living over a cavern . . . (*Crosses to bedroom off* L. *of Dorothea. Isabel crosses* U. *to dinette, and turns off living room light. George sits in chair.*)

DOROTHEA. (*Turns.*) But Mama's took all my things! I forgot to ask them back from her.—I'll just have to sleep jay-bird since she took even my nighties..

RALPH. Yes, she was fast and thorough, but didn't get out with that seven hundred buck beaver coat.

DOROTHEA. I like your friends. But the girl looks terribly nervous. Well-bred, however, and the boy is certainly very good-looking! (*Pause.*)

RALPH. —thanks. (*Lies on bed. The bedroom dims out as Dorothea enters bathroom. A silence has fallen between the pair in the living room.*)

ISABEL. (*Re-enters, with cup, to* R. C.) Coffee, George?

GEORGE. No, thanks.

ISABEL. Moods change quickly, don't they?

GEORGE. Basic attitudes don't.

ISABEL. Yes, but it takes a long time to form basic attitudes and to know what they are, and meantime you just have to act according to moods.

GEORGE. Is that what you are acting according to, now?

ISABEL. I'm not acting according to any thing at all now, I —— (*She sits on pouf before the fireplace.*) I don't think she came back just for the coat. Do you?

GEORGE. (*Rises, crosses to bar.*) It's not my business. I don't have any opinion. If that was her reason, Ralph Bates will soon find it out.

ISABEL. Yes . . .

DOROTHEA. (*Re-enters: knocks on living room door then crosses front of bar.*) Excuse me, may I come in?

ISABEL. Oh, please.

DOROTHEA. (*Entering.*) Mama took all my *things!* Have you got an extra nightie that I could borrow?

ISABEL. (*Crosses to bag at sofa, gets blue nightie.*) Of course I have.

DOROTHEA. (*To George, at bar.*) I forgot to take anything back . . . Oh! How exquisite! No!—That's your honeymoon nightie. Just give me any old plain one!

ISABEL. Really, I have another one exactly like it. Please take it!

DOROTHEA. Are you sure?

ISABEL. I'm positive. You take it! (*Holds up another.*) See? The same thing exactly, just a different color. I gave you the blue one and kept the pink one for me.

DOROTHEA. Oh. Well, thank you so much.

ISABEL. If you'd prefer the pink one ——?

DOROTHEA. I'm delighted with the blue one! Well, g'night, you folks. Sweet dreams.

ISABEL. Merry Christmas. (*Dorothea returns to the dark bedroom. Ralph is prone and motionless on the bed. A tiny light spills from the bathroom door. Dorothea enters the bathroom and closes the door so the bedroom turns pitch-black.*)

GEORGE. (*Grimly.*) D'ya want me to go outside while you undress?

ISABEL. No, I, I!—I'm—just going to take off my *dress.* I—I, I— have a *slip* on, I —— (*She gives him a quick, scared look. The removal of her dress is almost panickily self-conscious and awkward.*)

GEORGE. (*Turns to her.*) Well.—Ralph and I have decided to ——

ISABEL. (*Fearfully.*) *What?!* (*Pause.*)

GEORGE. (*Finishes drink, then goes on.*) —Ralph and I have decided to go in the cattle business, near San Antone.

ISABEL. Who is going to finance it?

GEORGE. We think we can work it out. We have to be smart, and lucky. Just smart and lucky. (*Isabel drops skirt to her feet and stands before the flickering fireplace in a slip that the light makes transparent.*)

ISABEL. We all have to be smart and lucky.—Or unlucky and silly. (*Dorothea re-enters, crosses to dressing table, sits. Brushes hair.*)

RALPH. (*Rises between beds, shirt off.*) All right, you're back.

But a lot has been discussed and decided on since you cut out of here, Dotty.

DOROTHEA. GOOD —— WHAT? (*Picks up something on dresser.*)

RALPH. Please don't rub that Vick's Vap-o-Rub on your chest.

DOROTHEA. I'm *not!* This is Hind's honey-almond cream for my *hands!*

RALPH. Aw. (*Starts taking off shoes. In living room—*)

GEORGE. (*At bar.*) What're you up to?

ISABEL. Up to?

GEORGE. Standin' in front of that fire with that transparent thing on you. You must know it's transparent. (*Crosses out to porch.*)

ISABEL. I honestly didn't even think about that. (*Isabel crouches by fire, holding her delicate hands out to its faint, flickering glow. In bedroom—*)

RALPH. All right. Here it is. George and me are going to cash in every bit of collateral we possess, including the beaver skin coat and his fifty-two Caddy to buy a piece of ranch-land near San Antone.

DOROTHEA. Oh. What are you planning to do on this ——

RALPH. —Ranch? Breed cattle. Texas Long Horns. (*Pause.*)

DOROTHEA. I like animals, Ralph.

RALPH. Cocker spaniels.

DOROTHEA. No, I like horses, too. I took equitation at Sophie Newcomb's. (*George re-enters living room, crosses C., then crosses to bar, sits on stage stool.*) I even learned how to post.

RALPH. Uh-huh.

DOROTHEA. For a little ole Texas girl she sure does have some mighty French taste in nighties!

RALPH. I don't imagine she suffers from psychological frigidity.

DOROTHEA. Honey, I never suffered from that. Did you believe I really suffered from that?

RALPH. When your father proposed to me ——

DOROTHEA. Ralph, don't say things like that! Don't, don't humiliate me!

RALPH. (*Goes to her.*) Honey, I ——

DOROTHEA. (*Cries.*) PLEASE don't humiliate me by ——

RALPH. (*Puts arms around her.*) HONEY! You KNOW I respect you, honey. Honey, will you stop?

DOROTHEA. Respect me, respect me, is that all you can give me when I've loved you so much that sometimes I shake all over at the sight or touch of you!? Still? Now? Always? (*He backs up* R.)

ISABEL. (*In other room.*) What an awful, frightening thing it is!

GEORGE. What?

ISABEL. Two people living together, two, two—different worlds! —attempting—existence—together!

RALPH. The human heart would never pass the drunk-test.

DOROTHEA. Huh?

RALPH. If you took the human heart out of the human body and put a pair of legs on it and told it to walk a straight line, it couldn't do it. It never could pass the drunk-test.

DOROTHEA. (*Hugs him.*) I love you, baby. And I love animals, too. Hawses, spaniels, long-horns!!

RALPH. The Texas long-horn is a—dignified beast.

DOROTHEA. You say that like you thought it was TOO GOOD FOR ME!

RALPH. (*Breaks away.*) How do I know that you didn't just come back here for that sheared beaver coat?

DOROTHEA. You'll just have to WONDER! And WONDER!

RALPH. All my life, huh?

ISABEL. I hope they're getting things ironed out between them.

GEORGE. (*Rises, crosses* D.) Why?

ISABEL. They need each other. That's why.

GEORGE. (*Above her.*) Let's mind our own business, huh?

DOROTHEA. And I'll have to wonder, too, if you love me, Ralph. There's an awful lot of wondering between people.

GEORGE. (*Sits arm of chair.*) It's a parallel situation. They're going through a period of adjustment just like us.

RALPH. (*They embrace.*) Come on. Let's go to bed-ville, baby.

DOROTHEA. His or hers? (*George crosses* D. *to turn on* TV. *Crosses* U. *again.*)

RALPH. In west Texas we'll get a big one called OURS! (*They kiss. On* TV—*chorus is singing another "White Christmas."*) [*Sound No. 24*]

GEORGE. (*Crosses* D., *turns off* TV. *Then crosses* U. *to bar.*) Aw. You hate "White Christmas."

ISABEL. I don't hate it now, baby.

DOROTHEA. I'm looking *forward* to it. I always wanted a big one, OURS!

RALPH. There's more dignity in it.

DOROTHEA. (*Reclines on* D. *bed.*) Yes! (*She giggles breathlessly in the dark.*)

RALPH. Yes. It makes it easy to know if—I mean, you don't have to wonder if —— (*Dorothea giggles in the dark. He crosses to door.*) That long, long, dangerous walk between "His" and "Hers" can be accomplished, or not . . . (*He exits to bathroom, turns off light.*)

ISABEL. (*George crosses* D. *to sofa.*) I think they've talked things over and are working things out. . . . I didn't know until now that the shakes are catching! (*He rises, crosses* U. R.) Why do you keep standing up and sitting back down like a big old jack-in-the-box? (*A low rumble is heard. It builds. Something falls off a shelf in the kitchenette. Crockery rattles together. [Sound No. 25] Isabel jumps up into George's arms. Ralph pokes head into bedroom, then Dorothea crosses into living room. Isabel and George break.*) WHAT'S THAT!?

RALPH. (*Entering doorway.*) Well, she jus' slipped again!

DOROTHEA. Did you all feel that tremor?

ISABEL. Yes, it felt like an earthquake.

DOROTHEA. (D. *of bar.* Isabel *at* L. C. George U. C.) We get those little tremors all the time because it seems that this suburb is built over a huge underground cavern and is sinking into it, bit by bit. That's the secret of how we could afford to buy this nice little home of ours at such a knock-down price.

ISABEL. It isn't likely to fall in the cavern tonight?

DOROTHEA. No. They say it's going to be gradual, about half an inch every year. Do you all mind if I turn on the light a second to see if there's any new cracks?

ISABEL. No, I'll—put on my robe. (*She does and crosses* R. *above chair. The lights go on.*)

DOROTHEA. (*Steps down, looks up.*) Yais! Ralph? A new one! This one is a jim-dandy, all the way 'cross the ceiling! (*He enters in pajamas, to her* R.) See it, honey? All the way 'cross the ceiling. Well —— (*Pause. She moves stool to bar.*) We will leave you alone now. I still feel badly about you having to sleep on that folding contraption. (*Exits to bathroom to get pillows. Ralph sets up bed—gets pillows from Dottie.*)

RALPH. (*Crosses* U. *to George.*) Anything I can do? Anything I can —— (*George shakes head.*)

DOROTHEA. Ralph! Leave them alone. Merry Christmas! (*Pause.*

Isabel stands before fireplace in the fourth wall. Pause. Dorothea crosses to bedroom, then Ralph crosses to bedroom. She gets into u. bed after turning out table lamp. Ralph crosses into bathroom.)

GEORGE. (*Crossing to sofa.*) Isabel? Little Bit? Marriage is a big step for a man to take, especially when he's—nervous. I'm pretty—nervous.

ISABEL. I know.

GEORGE. For a man with the shakes, especially, it's a—big step to take ——

ISABEL. I know what you're trying to tell me, George.

GEORGE. (*Taking seat on high stool near fire.*) Do you, honey? (*He looks up at her quickly, then down.*)

ISABEL. Of course I do. I expect all men are a little bit nervous about the same thing.

GEORGE. What?

ISABEL. About how they'll be at love-making.

GEORGE. —Yeah, well, they don't have the shakes. I mean, not all the others have got a nervous tremor like I've got.

ISABEL. Inside or outside, they've all got a nervous tremor of some kind, sweetheart. The world is a big hospital, and I am a nurse in it, George. The whole world's a big hospital, a big neurological ward and I am a student nurse in it. I guess that's still my job!—I love this fire. It feels so good on my skin through this little pink slip. I'm glad she left me the pink nightie, tonight.

GEORGE. (*Huskily.*) So am I.—I wish I had that—little electric buzzer I—had at—Barnes . . .

ISABEL. You don't need a buzzer. I'm not way down at the end of a corridor, baby. If you call me, I'll hear you. (*She returns and hugs her knees, sitting before the fireplace. He rests his head on his cupped hands. She begins to sing softly—*)

> "Now the boat goes round the bend,
> Goodbye, my lover, goodbye,
> It's loaded down with boys and men,
> Goodbye, my lover, goodbye!"

RALPH. (*Re-enters to door of bedroom. In the dark other room.*) She's singin'! (*Pause. He gets into bed.*)

DOROTHEA. Papa said you told him that I was—homely! Did you say that, Ralph? That I was homely?

RALPH. Dotty, you used to be homely but you improved in appearance.

DOROTHEA. You never told me you thought I was homely, Ralph.

RALPH. I just meant you had a off-beat kind of face, honey, but ——

DOROTHEA. (*Giggles.*) I always knew *I* was homely but you were good enough lookin' to make *up* for it! Baby —— (*Isabel singing again, a little forlornly, by the fireplace.*)

ISABEL. "Bye low, my baby! Bye low, my baby!
Bye low, my baby! Goodbye, my lover, goodbye!"
(*George makes tentative gesture, then whistles.*) Was that for me?

GEORGE. Would you come here!

ISABEL. No, you come here. It's very nice by the fire. (*She extends her hand. He rises, crosses to her, takes her hand. In other room, as the curtain begins to fall—*)

DOROTHEA. Careful, let me do it!—It isn't mine! (*Means the borrowed nightgown. In front room, George has risen from bed and is crossing to fireplace as—*)

THE CURTAIN FALLS

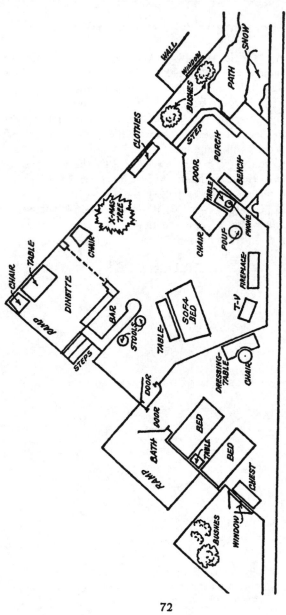

SCENE DESIGN

"PERIOD OF ADJUSTMENT"

DESIGNED BY
JO MIELZINER
COPYRIGHT 1960

Bedroom

Chest—D. R. on it—small brush, lamp D. S. "Infant of Prague" statuette (penny under it) U. S.

In drawers—women's clothing

Twin beds—"His" and "Her" plaques over beds
  Note: "His" bed U S.

Table between beds—on it—phone, ashtray

Twin lamps over table

Dressing table D. L.—on it—ladies hand mirror, hair brush, comb, jar of cream (practical), another jar of cream (not practical), atomizer, ashtray, vanity box, powder jar

Stool at table

Light switch at door

Dressing room—off right

Rod—on it—"His' and "Her" towels

Table—on it—2 cologne bottles

Living room

Bar—on it— ice bucket, ashtray, 2 cocktail and 2 highball glasses, cocktail shaker, mixing glass and spoon, ashtray, beer can opener, drink strainer, bottle (cork) opener, beer can opener, can of beer (filled one-half full with water), box of matches, china ashtray

Shelf below bar—2 cans of beer (one-half full of water), bar rag, leather bar case, 3 cans of beer (three-fourths full of water), matches

Back of bar—bottle of gin, highball glass, brandy

  1st shelf—inhaler, bottle of Kentucky bourbon, brandy inhaler, highball glass, bottle of rye

  2nd shelf—bottle of Haig & Haig, champagne glass, brass cannon, champagne glass, bottle of Kentucky bourbon

  3rd shelf—figurette, loving cup with flags, figurette

2 bar stools

Light switch O. S. end of bar

Modern hanging lamp over bar

Picture (breakaway) on wall D. R. of bar

Dinette

Table—on it—tablecloth, Japanese doll, box of rice (practical)

Hanging shelf with 4 plates U. S. wall

Aunt Jemima (doll pad) on R. wall
Chair R. of table
Hanging lantern above table
Dog leash D. S. side of arch

Living room
Christmas tree U. L. C.—decorated—tree lights
Under tree—on red cloth—rocking horse, chemistry set, cowboy outfit, alphabet blocks, tunnel, rocket launcher, Xmas box, train station, beaver skin coat in box, train set
Chair R. of tree
Dog basket L. of tree
Hall tree above door L.
    On it—man's mackinaw, man's sweater, umbrella and rubbers
Spike for dog leash between halltree & dog basket
Armchair below door L.
Table L. of it on it—phone, china ashtray below phone, glass ashtray above phone, matches
Fireplace D. C.—logs, asbestos ashtray, box of tapers, fire broom, bellows, poker
Pouf L. of fire on mark
TV set R. of fire on it—brass ashtray
Castro sofa R. (made up with sheet & blanket for Act III)
Table back of sofa—on it—3 Xmas boxes, string of Xmas tree lights, bottle of brandy (practical, Xmas wrapped)
Bar stool D. C. on mark
Wall brackets R. & L. of tree and over picture D. R. of bar

Porch
Knocker on door
Wreath on door
Bench D. R.
Kiddie car U. L.
String of lights & hanging lamp
Light switch
Snow shovel R. of garage door
2 trees R. & L. of garage door
Tree outside window in Bedroom off D. R.

ACT I

HAND PROPS

Handkerchief (Ralph)
Wristwatch (Ralph)

Off Left
3 blue traveling cases (1 large, 1 medium, and 1 small)
In small case ("blue zipper bag")—1 pink nightgown, 1 blue night-
    gown (Dorothea), robe and slippers (Isabel), mirror, comb, brush,
    2 bottles of cologne, bottle of "Vol de Nuit" in box
Bottle of champagne (George)
Check "snowflakes" and "dust"

ACT II

Check glass of brandy at u. s. end of phone table
4 cans of beer at bar
Set 2 cans (three-fourths full) and champagne on stool c.
Car keys (George)
Move pouf to below phone table
Move c. stool to mark
Strike rice box to dinette table
Strike brandy box from bar
Strike Isabel's purse, gloves, and Xmas lights
Rewire picture

Off Right
Pepto-bismol (practical, milkshake) and spoon
Glass of water
Terry cloth robe and slippers (Isabel)

ACT III

Champagne bottle (open-practical) and 2 champagne glasses on dinette
    table
Door key (Dorothea)
Cigar and matches (Mr. McGillicuddy)
Check open fur box on sofa table
Check two ashtrays on phone table
Place Isabel's jacket and scarf from hook to shelf on halltree
Strike brandy glass, Pepto-bismol, water glass from dressing table
Terry robe and slippers from bed

Off Left
Large laundry basket (Susie)
Shopping bag (Mrs. McGillicuddy)

Off Right
Porcelain clock, 6 dresses (Mrs. McGillicuddy)
Silver-ware in cloth case (George)
2 pillows in dressing room

Pajamas and slippers (Ralph)
Slippers (Dorothea)
2 cups of coffee on tray
1 cup of coffee

WARDROBE PLOT

RALPH
Blue and white check knit shirt w/collar
Dark brown unpleated slacks
Tan low desert shoes
Light brown socks
White handkerchief
White tee shirt

GEORGE
White tee shirt
Dark blue sport shirt
Light brown corduroy pants
Tan desert boots
Dark blue socks
Brown short leather jacket

ISABEL
1 beige dress, zip up back, short sleeve, V collar
1 jacket for dress
1 white cloth coat with white fur collar
White gloves
White handbag
Full white slip
Nylon stockings
High heel shoes (same color as dress)
Terry cloth bathrobe
White puff house slippers
Sheer robe

DOROTHEA
Long sleeved green blouse
Grey pleated skirt
Red/brown flecked cloth coat
Brown shoulder handbag
Blue nightgown

MR. MCGILLICUDDY
Camel hair double breasted overcoat
Brown felt hat

Dark double breasted suit
Vest
White shirt
Pattern necktie
Jeweled stickpin
Brown shoes
Brown socks

MRS. McGILLICUDDY
Red cloth coat
Stole martin (fur)
Red wool suit
  Skirt
  Jacket
White blouse
Red feather hat
Nylon stockings
Black shoes
Black handbag
Black gloves
Ring
Bracelets
SUSIE
Blue uniform
Short grey jacket
Stockings
Brown loafers

POLICEMAN
Blue jacket, badge
Blue pants
Police cap, badge
Black shoes
Black socks
White shirt
Black tie

SOUND PLOT